FOLK MUSIC

THE BASICS

- Gives a concise history of folk music in the United States and the British Isles, 1800–2000
- Presents a basic but comprehensive introduction for both students and folk music fans
- Highlights key performers, including Pete Seeger, Woody Guthrie, Bob Dylan, and many more

Folk Music: The Basics offers an introduction to two hundred years of British and American folk music. It is a fresh approach to various aspects of folk music, including collectors and scholars, amateurs as well as professional performers, transatlantic influences, the changing nature of public acceptance, and much more. The two sides of the folk tradition are examined—both as popular and commercial expressions. Throughout, sidebars offer studies of key folk performers, record labels, and related issues to place the general discussion in context. A comprehensive bibliography and discography provide resources for further research.

Folk Music: The Basics serves as an excellent introduction to the players, the music, and the styles that make folk music an enduring and well-loved musical style.

Ronald D. Cohen is Emeritus Professor of History at Indiana University Northwest. He is a well-known authority on folk music, and the author of *Rainbow Quest: The Folk Music Revival* and *American Society, 1940–1970,* among other works.

You may also be interested in the following Routledge Student Reference titles:

BLUES: THE BASICS
Dick Weissman

JAZZ: THE BASICS
Christopher Meeder

OPERA: THE BASICS
Denise Gallo

WORLD MUSIC: THE BASICS
Richard Nidel

FOLK MUSIC
THE BASICS

ronald d. cohen

Routledge
Taylor & Francis Group
New York   London

Routledge is an imprint of the
Taylor & Francis Group, an informa business

Published in 2006 by
Routledge
Taylor & Francis Group
270 Madison Avenue
New York, NY 10016

Published in Great Britain by
Routledge
Taylor & Francis Group
2 Park Square
Milton Park, Abingdon
Oxon OX14 4RN

© 2006 by Taylor & Francis Group, LLC
Routledge is an imprint of Taylor & Francis Group

Printed in the United States of America on acid-free paper
10 9 8 7 6 5 4 3 2 1

International Standard Book Number-10: 0-415-97159-4 (Hardcover) 0-415-97160-8 (Softcover)
International Standard Book Number-13: 978-0-415-97159-1 (Hardcover) 978-0-415-97160-7 (Softcover)
Library of Congress Card Number 2005030520

Library of Congress Cataloging-in-Publication Data

Cohen, Ronald D., 1940-
    Folk music : the basics / Ronald D. Cohen.
        p. cm. -- (The basics) (Routledge student reference)
    Includes bibliographical references (p.   ), discography (p.   ), and index.
    ISBN 0-415-97159-4 (hb) -- ISBN 0-415-97160-8 (pb)
    1. Folk music--United States--History and criticism. 2. Folk music—Great Britain--History and criticism. I. Title. II. Series. III. Series: Basics (Routledge (Firm))

ML3551.C578 2006
781.6200973'0904--dc22   2005030520

Taylor & Francis Group
is the Academic Division of Informa plc.

Visit the Taylor & Francis Web site at
http://www.taylorandfrancis.com

and the Routledge Web site at
http://www.routledge-ny.com

CONTENTS

INTRODUCTION

Folk Music: The Basics is designed as an introduction to the history of folk music in Great Britain and the United States, concentrating on the nineteenth and twentieth centuries. I have drawn upon a wide range of sources, with the most helpful and important books listed in the bibliography, including the previously published *Blues: The Basics* by Dick Weissman. I have also added a discography of selected CDs, most of which should be currently available.

The student today has the good fortune to have available much of the recorded folk music of the twentieth century, so that the music is more than an abstraction. Of course, folk music can be variously defined, and I have tried a realistic interpretation in Chapter 1, although my later discussion might not always adhere to my own self-imposed musical limits. I explore these developments in both Great Britain and the United States, and in the process trace the strong historical connections and influences between the two, which I hope is my contribution to the ongoing literature. There has been a similar folk music history in Canada, but unfortunately space prevents discussing this fascinating topic, which still needs its historian.

Folk music has always been around, but has not always had a large, popular following. Technological breakthroughs in the twentieth century, such as the phonograph, radio, and television, have made it possible to reach a wide audience, promoting the commercial outgrowth of folk music, broadly defined. These developments continue into the twenty-first century, making readily available an amazing variety of folk styles, old and new, including, most recently, world music.

I hope what follows will acquaint the reader with the rich and complex history of the topic, as an introduction to enjoying not only folk music of the past, but also of the present and into the future. I have only covered the tip of the folk music iceberg, and there is much more work to be done, as the current proliferation of scholarly studies demonstrates—check the bibliography for these recent publications. Folk music has had a strong appeal, perhaps even mystical, for traditional rural people and urban dwellers alike for many centuries, even as it has gone through various incarnations and transformations. This book is a partial attempt to describe and understand this historical situation and process.

I want to thank Ed Cray, Millie Rahn, Bob Riesman, David Gregory, and particularly my editor and inspiration at Routledge, Richard Carlin, for their most helpful suggestions, comments, and corrections, which have greatly assisted to make this book as readable and accurate as possible. Any errors or misinterpretations are entirely the fault of the author. I also want to thank all of those who have assisted me in the past, since I have drawn upon many years of researching the history of folk music—check the notes to my earlier study, *Rainbow Quest: The Folk Music Revival and American Society, 1940–1970*. Still, there is much more to do. And last, I again want to acknowledge my partner, Nancy, for her love and support, always needed and welcomed.

NINETEENTH CENTURY BACKGROUND
Great Britain and the United States

DEFINITIONS

It might appear simple to understand folk music as a form of popular music in the British Isles and the United States with antique roots and anonymous composers. But in order to understand the scope and transformation of folk music through the nineteenth and twentieth centuries, it is necessary to come up with a broader definition. For example, we will have to include in our story not only the development and collection of old songs, with no known composers, but also labor songs of the nineteenth century broadsides, blues, gospel tunes, cowboy songs, singer/songwriters, such as Donovan and Bob Dylan, who emerged in the 1960s, and so much more. We shall attempt to come up with a narrative history that is all inclusive, but also one that will establish some limits on what should be included or excluded. For example, jazz, opera, and, usually, commercially written popular songs will be excluded. In its traditional form, folk music can be said to include the following attributes: (1) its origins can perhaps be located in a particular culture or region; (2) authorship has historically been unknown,

although authors did emerge over the past two centuries;
(3) it has traditionally been performed by nonprofession-
als, perhaps playing acoustic instruments; (4) its composition has been fairly simple, with perhaps little complexity
so that it can be performed and shared communally; and (5)
the songs have historically been passed down through oral
transmission. This has somewhat changed, particularly if
we include the rise of the cheap print media, and, in the
twentieth century, the introduction of phonograph records,
radio and television shows, films, and concerts. That is, folk
music has been the music of the people, broadly construed,
although this might seem too simplistic.

Folk music has encompassed various musical styles. One
form has been the *ballad*, which is essentially a story song
written in a narrative style. Folklorists, those who study
cultural traditions, have been particularly interested in discovering and interpreting ballads, which seemed to have
given insights into particular older societies. There have
been two different kinds of traditional ballads, one coming from a remote past with an anonymous author, and the
other coming from published broadsides, printed sheets
with words but no music, beginning in the sixteenth century, often with known authors who were commenting
on contemporary events and individuals. The former were
preserved through oral transmission over a long period
of time, and can be associated with *vernacular* (or common) culture, while most of the latter had a short public
life and did not necessarily enter into common usage, but
some did. In the nineteenth century there also developed
the blues ballad among African Americans in the American South, usually based on personal relationships or local
events. The other general type of folk song has had no story
line, but a series of lyrics that were often catchy, and perhaps included rhyming lyrics. Some might relate to work
experiences, personal relationships, life and death, patriotic feelings, or children's games, in a religious or secular

context. Folk songs traditionally have not had a commercial origin, although such songs composed for a popular audience, could have, and often did, eventually enter into a folk consciousness within a few generations. We can also make a distinction between performers whose family roots were in traditional music, and those outsiders who have picked up and carried on traditional songs and styles. Born into an upper-class family, Pete Seeger, for example, has emphasized the distinction, noting that he is not a folk singer, but a singer of folk songs.

In the twentieth century, folk music took on a much wider meaning, and the traditional definitions had to be reconsidered. Traditional ballads, either narrative, blues, or broadside, as well as lyric songs continued, but were joined by nineteenth-century popular songs and then an increasing number of singer/songwriters, gospel songs, and much more that became part of the expanding, flexible understanding of folk music. Instrumental accompaniment also broadened, from acoustic guitar, banjo, fiddle, harmonica, and mandolin, to eventually include electric guitars, brass, and percussion instruments, and just about anything else. Moreover, while music from the British Isles and Africa have appeared to be the basic sources of folk music in the United States, peoples from various European countries and other parts of the world transported their music to the New World, where it has mixed with the dominant styles. An understanding of folk music in both the British Isles and the United States from the nineteenth to the twentieth centuries, therefore, will have to include a flexible, expanding definition that leads to a narrowing of the gaps between folk, popular music, and what is now labeled as world music. This understanding will become clearer as this fascinating story unfolds.

NINETEENTH CENTURY IN BRITISH ISLES: COLLECTORS AND SONGS

Folk song collecting has had a long and rich history in England and Scotland, and by the end of the nineteenth century there existed a large body of published collections. Thomas D'Urfey edited six volumes of *Wit and Mirth* or *Pills to Purge Melancholy* (1719–1720), containing over one thousand verses of ballads and poems, drawn mostly from various published collections, broadsides, books of poetry, and his own compositions. While the majority were not gathered from oral traditions, some could be considered folk songs, while most were initially popular songs. A few years later (1723–1725) *A Collection of Old Ballads* appeared in three volumes, again based mostly on published broadsides and earlier collections. Later in the century Thomas Percy's *Reliques of Ancient English Poetry* (1765) helped initiate the ballad revival. Joseph Ritson published *A Select Collection of English Songs in Three Volumes* (1783), also composed mainly of published poems and songs, found in broadsides or manuscript collections, including both words and music. Simultaneously, various collections of ballads appeared in Scotland, including the songs and poems of Robert Burns, for example in George Thomson's *The Scots Musical Museum* (1771). Of perhaps greater importance was Sir Walter Scott's *Minstrelsy of the Scottish Border* (1802–1803), mostly drawn from manuscript collections. Publishing ballad and folksong collections increased throughout the nineteenth century. Again, most were drawn from published broadside and manuscript collections, although there was a gradual increase in field collecting. William Chappell published a variety of influential collections, particularly *Popular Music of the Olden Time* (1858–1859), a massive two-volume compilation, which included "Greensleeves" and various tunes drawn from Shakespeare's plays, as well as the anonymous "Barbara Allen," which he seems to have drawn from oral tradition. Chronologically arranged, and including both words and music, beginning with Anglo-Saxon melodies, Chappell's work drew upon an array of manuscript and published collections, as well as scores of broadside and Robin Hood ballads. While he found a few in oral tradition, the vast majority of the selections had not been passed down to the mid-nineteenth century; that is, they were not currently performed. But *Popular Music of the Olden Time* served as a valuable reference work for later scholars. By century's end, there were also a myriad of cheap popular songsters, containing a rich array of tunes, including Scottish vernacular songs such as "Green Grow the Rashes O" and "Annie Laurie," and even a few from the United States, such as Stephen Foster's "The Old Folks at Home."

Ballad and folk song collecting accelerated through the end of the nineteenth century. On the regional level, Davison Ingledew's *The Ballads and Songs of Yorkshire* (1860), John Harland's *Ballads and Songs of Lancashire* (1865), and Thomas Allan's *Tyneside Songs* (1891) added significantly to an awareness of local traditions. They were joined by William Allingham's *The Ballad Book* (1864) bringing together English and Scottish traditional ballads. W. H. Logan and Joseph Ebsworth reprinted numerous ballads and other older songs, including Logan's *A Pedlar's Pack of Ballads and Songs* (1869), and the extensive work of William Chappell. Carl Engel's *The Literature of National Music* (1879) stimulated field collecting of folk songs; Charlotte Burne, for example, discovered numerous contemporary singers in the West Midlands, *Shropshire Folk-Lore* (1883–1886). Sabine Baring-Gould, a parson in Devon, collected and published songs from numerous singers. Other late Victorian field collectors found far fewer sources; Lucy Broadwood, for example, collected from about 35 individuals, while Frank Kidson had even fewer informants. Broadwood, along with J. A. Fuller Maitland, published *English Country Songs, Words and Music* (1893), while Kidson issued *Traditional Tunes:*

A Collection of Ballad Airs, Chiefly Obtained in Yorkshire and the South of Scotland (1891). The Percy Society early in the century, and the Ballad Society by the mid-late Victorian era, assisted in promoting a broader interest in traditional ballads and songs, leading to the founding of the English Folk Song Society in 1898.

By the end of the nineteenth century, therefore, there existed a rich variety of ballad and folk song collections by English and Scottish collectors and publishers, easily accessible for scholars and the general public. Many drew upon earlier chapbooks or garlands (other names for songbooks), as well as broadsides (single sheets that were individually sold by ballad singers or peddlers in the cities or roving about the countryside). There were ballads on crimes and criminals, victories at sea, border raids, and murders most foul. Many dealt with love and sex; there was even a body of bawdy songs, some verging on the obscene, that circulated in oral tradition.

It remained for an American professor, however, to publish what would remain the standard collection of British and Scottish ballads. Francis James Child's prime achievement was his edition of five volumes of *The English and Scottish Popular Ballads* (1882–1898), which established the benchmark for ballad collecting through the following century in both the British Isles and the United States. Born in Boston, Massachusetts, Child (1825–1896) was a professor of medieval studies and English literature at Harvard College who developed a singular interest in British ballads. Researching both published and manuscript sources (he did no fieldwork), he finally published numerous variations of 305 ballads. He focused on what he thought to be ancient ballads of a rather impersonal nature, which can be divided into four categories: magical and marvelous, romantic and tragic, historical and legendary, or humorous; a man of his Victorian times, he refused to publish any with bawdy lyrics, however.

The romantic and tragic, often encompassing love affairs, seem to have been the most popular, particularly in the United States. Child included, among many others, "Mary Hamilton" (173), "Lord Bateman" (53) "Lord Thomas and Fair Annet" (73), and "Bonny Barbara Allan" (84). Child also helped found the American Folklore Society in 1888 (patterned on The Folklore Society, founded in England in 1878) and served as its first president.

Ballads and songs relating to industrial work proliferated through the nineteenth century. Many exhibited anger and resistance to the transformation of the work place. "The Hand-Loom Weavers' Lament" is an attack on the new factory owners and the loss of a market for traditional skills and independence. On the other hand, some broadsides celebrated factory life and factory towns, such as "Oldham Workshops." Musician and folklorist A. L. Lloyd (1967) describes the legitimate "industrial folk song" as "the kind of vernacular songs made by workers themselves directly out of their own experience, expressing their own interests and aspirations, and incidentally passed on among themselves mainly by oral means" (p. 317). He includes "The Poor Cotton Weaver," "Poverty Knock," and "The Coal-Owner and the Pitman's Wife" as examples in this category. There were also numerous professionally written music-hall songs dealing with workers' lives, which, while not initially folk songs, could eventually be considered of a vernacular nature. Joe Wilson's "The Strike" falls into this category, dealing with the work stoppage in 1871 to obtain a nine-hour day in the Tyneside.

Throughout the nineteenth century traditional ballads and folk songs circulated through the British Isles, some passed along through family and community oral traditions, others by way of published books, songsters, and broadsides. In addition, there were a growing number of urban, industrial, and maritime songs that would become part of the folk legacy that stretched through the twentieth century.

Street literature, in the form of broadsides, flourished in urban areas. Ballads and songs had long captured personal feelings, violence, and tragedies, such as "The Golden Vanity" and "The Sheffield Apprentice," but had begun to take on more contemporary stories about common people by the early nineteenth century, often sprinkled with humorous passages. Traditional singers focused on a song's words, while broadside sellers performed for a crowd in order to attract buyers, who were often young people looking for romance or adventure. Communities and trade unions had their own bards, who crafted verse for various occasions.

On the eve of the twentieth century there existed a rich and ever-expanding legacy of ballads and folksongs in the British Isles, performed locally and increasingly collected by scholars and interested antiquarians, who formed the Folk-Song Society in 1898 to promote future collecting and publications.

NINETEENTH CENTURY IN THE UNITED STATES: COLLECTORS AND SONGS

Folk songs and ballads in the United States in the nineteenth century somewhat followed the British style, but there were significant variations because of racial, ethnic, economic, and geographical diversity. By the early nineteenth century there existed a diverse body of folk music throughout the country, heavily influenced by both British and African musical styles, and often with a religious message. In addition, as immigrants from European countries began arriving in large numbers by midcentury they brought their own music and songs, as did those Mexican citizens whose lands in the Southwest had been incorporated into the country, as well as the Native Americans. By century's end there existed a vast array of musical forms and styles, much of which could be (or would later be) classified under the folk music rubric.

British, which included Scottish and Irish, as well as native songs and ballads were common throughout the United States by the mid-nineteenth century. There were also other forms of folk songs, including play party songs, such as "Skip to My Lou" and "Get Along Home, Cindy," which originally were accompanied by singing and hand clapping, but not musical instruments. There were also numerous fiddle tunes, for example "Soldier's Joy" and "Old Joe Clark." Just as in Britain, songs circulated through oral means as well as in published forms—broadsides, songsters, and sheet music. British influences were common. Songs and ballads were transported either wholesale to the New World, or influenced American versions. For example, the melody of "The Cowboy's Lament" (also known as "The Streets of Laredo") originated originally in Ireland as "The Bard of Armagh" (later the nationalist tune "Bold Robert Emmet"), while "Sweet Betsy from Pike" started as "The Ould Orange Flute." Few ballads survived in oral traditions from the eighteenth century, such as "On Springfield Mountain" and "Brave Wolfe," and others in the Child canon.

In the nineteenth century, ballads and folk songs were newly written and often related to various occupations and experiences, such as lumbermen and sailors. These occupations produced what were called shanties, such as "Blow the Man Down," "Reuben Ranzo," "Shenandoah," and "Blow, Boys, Blow," which derived from long months at sea, while "The Jam on Gerry's Rock," "The Lumber Camp Song," and "The Lumberman's Alphabet" came from life in the North woods. Sea shanties were the work songs of sailors on the sailing ships, while in the logging camps, "shanty" referred to the primitive housing conditions; a "shantyboy" was another name for a woodsman or lumberjack. There were two kinds of sailor songs: work songs that paced various group efforts on the sailing ships, and forecastle songs that were sung for entertainment, which could include ribald verses.

Indeed, songs connected to various occupations were common throughout the country. There were numerous railroad songs, such as "Casey Jones," miners songs, cowboy songs, and others connected with work experiences. "Buddy Won't You Roll Down the Line," "The Coal Creek Rebellion," and "Miner's Lifeguard," for example, resulted from various miners' upheavals in the 1890s and later were considered folk songs. Most labor-connected songs at the time, however, related to particular events, such as the eight-hour day movement in Chicago in the 1880s, or the Homestead strike in Pennsylvania and the Pullman Palace Car company strike in the 1890s, and were quickly forgotten. Various farmer and labor organizations, such as the Knights of Labor and the Socialist Labor Party, also generated numerous songs that also did not enter into the broader collective musical memory.

Beginning in the seventeenth century and continuing into the nineteenth, millions of slaves were brought from Africa to the New World. They brought with them traditional musical styles and instruments, including the prototype of the banjo and various drums, and by the Civil War (1860–1865) the music of African Americans, both slave and free, was common. Work songs, including field hollers and urban street cries, and religious tunes or spirituals predominated. William Allen, Charles Ware, and Lucy McKim Garrison published *Slave Songs of the United States* in 1867, a seminal collection that documented African-American songs at a time when there was little interest in publishing collections of European or indigenous white folk songs in the country. Allen began collecting songs while teaching in ex-slave schools in South Carolina in late 1863, while the Civil War still raged, and later taught at Antioch College and the University of Wisconsin. This landmark book included musical scores for the 136 selections, including work songs, spirituals, dance and play songs, ballads, satirical songs, and street cries. Also in 1867 Thomas Wentworth Higginson

GUITAR AND BANJO

Various instruments have been part of folk music performance in both Great Britain and the Unites States, perhaps most important being the guitar and banjo, beginning in the nineteenth century. The six-string guitar was developed in southern Europe in the late eighteenth century and quickly reached the United States. Manufacturing gut-string guitars began in the country in the 1830s, with the C. F. Martin Company leading the way, followed by Epiphone, Harmony, and Gibson. Steel-string instruments, originally from Central America, began to appear in the 1890s, with cheap models soon available in the Montgomery Ward and Sears, Roebuck catalogs. The mass production of guitars led to their use among rural musicians in the South, "where traveling black railroad workers often introduced [the guitar] to white mountaineers," historian Nolan Porterfield has noted. "Combined with the fiddle and banjo, the guitar added rhythmic accompaniment; moreover, its chords provided a solid background for singing, thus encouraging string bands to include songs as well as instrumentals in their repertoires." String bands, anchored by the guitar, were popular by the 1920s, but soon influential personal styles emerged, led by Jimmie Rodgers and Maybelle Carter. Since the 1930s the guitar has become the most important instrument in many aspects of popular music, with both a lead and rhythm function, including country, folk, jazz, and certainly rock. Variations include the Hawaiian and Dobro resonator guitars, which are played with a slide or bottleneck. The electric guitar was invented in the 1930s. Both electric and acoustic guitars have had extensive sales into the twenty-first century.

A stringed instrument was brought to the New World by West African slaves by the eighteenth century, which evolved into the banjo. The number of strings varied, from three to eight, with four the early standard. A short fifth string was added before the Civil War, and this model eventually became more popular among rural musicians. White minstrel performers in blackface adapted the banjo to their widely popular entertainment, and following the Civil War, it had lost much of its association with African Americans. By the end of the nineteenth century the machine-made banjo, led by the Fairbanks, Cole, and Vega companies, was widely popular, with banjo (as well as mandolin and guitar) clubs springing up throughout the country. The four-string style was developed and used in ragtime and early jazz bands, while the five-string was known more as a folk instrument in the rural South. By the 1920s Uncle Dave Macon was established on the Grand Ole Opry radio show as a flamboyant banjo player, although the instrument was more common in the string bands that proliferated at the time. Following World War II the banjo became less popular in country music, except for its role in shaping bluegrass music through the influence of Earl Scruggs. In urban folk music, however, it gained a prominent role, particularly through the playing of Pete Seeger, whose recordings and banjo instruction book, first self-published in 1948, were highly influential. The banjo assumed a prominent role with the emergence of the folk music revival in the 1950s, which continued through the century.

The guitar and banjo were only two of the instruments that have been used by folk musicians in the United States and Great Britain. Others have been the accordion, dulcimer, fiddle, harmonica, mandolin, mouth bow, washboard, tin whistle, concertina, drums, flute, harp, uilleann pipes, and others. Indeed, anything that can make a sound can be considered a folk instrument.

published a path-breaking article on "Negro Spirituals" in the *Atlantic Monthly*, a popular northern magazine.

Jubilee Songs as Sung by the Fisk Jubilee Singers was published in 1872, establishing another benchmark in promoting black music. The Fisk Jubilee Singers launched their first northern tour in 1871, designed to raise funds for the all-black Fisk University in Nashville, and in the process spread the popularity of African-American spirituals. The tour started slowly, but soon generated considerable attention; the group traveled through the North and Europe for the next seven years to growing acclaim. They were soon joined by the Hampton Singers, from the Hampton Institute in Virginia, in spreading far and wide authentic black spirituals, but with European-style arrangements, such as "Go Down Moses." Black fiddle and banjo (but not yet guitar) players were common throughout the nineteenth-century South, performing folk tunes from the British Isles with an African inflection, often for white dances. Indeed, white and black musicians influenced each other, a situation that increased through the twentieth century.

White audiences initially had difficulty appreciating black spirituals because they were used to white minstrel songs that appeared to represent authentic African-American musical forms and styles, but were in fact white creations and parodies. Beginning in the 1840s, and continuing through the century and into the next, minstrel shows featured whites in blackface makeup and included songs and dances, jokes, as well as satirical speeches and skits. Composers Dan Emmett and Stephen Foster turned out such compositions as "Dixie," "Camptown Races," "Oh! Susanna," and "My Old Kentucky Home" that soon became popular folk songs. Before the Civil War, minstrel shows were extremely popular in the North, and following the war black performers also put on blackface makeup and created their own minstrel acts. The black composer James Bland wrote for these shows "Oh, Dem Golden Slippers," "In the Evening by the Moonlight," and "Carry Me Back to Old Virginny," that also eventually entered the folk repertoire. Various African American ballads, such as "John Henry," "The Boll Weevil," "Frankie and Albert," and the pre–Civil War minstrel-style "The Blue-Tail Fly" also became mainstays of the folk repertoire and popular songbooks, while somewhat losing their racial designations.

Religious music among southern whites took various forms, including shape-note singing, based on a simplified musical notation that used various shapes, that appeared by 1800. Often using traditional folk melodies, shape-note tunebooks were widespread in religious services throughout the country; the most popular was *The Sacred Harp* by B. F. White and E. B. King (1844). Following the Civil War white gospel songs emerged, resulting in the publication of Ira Sankey and Philip Bliss, *Gospel Hymns and Sacred Songs* (1875), with numerous subsequent editions. They also often derived from folk styles, and quickly spread in churches around the country. Both shape-note and white gospel tunes later could be considered part of the larger world of folk music.

The Civil War produced a large number of popular songs, many of which eventually entered tradition. Among southern soldiers, "All Quiet Along the Potomac Tonight," "Annie Laurie," "The Girl I Left Behind Me," "Listen to the Mockingbird," "Just Before the Battle Mother," "Maryland, My Maryland," and particularly Dan Emmett's "Dixie" were favorites. While for northern troops Julia Ward Howe's "Battle Hymn of the Republic" (more popular as "John Brown's Body"), "The Battle Cry of Freedom," "When This Cruel War Is Over," "Marching Through Georgia," and "Tramp, Tramp, Tramp" were camp favorites.

Various instruments could be used for musical accompaniment, including the banjo, with the guitar and piano more limited until later. White musicians began to adopt the five-string banjo in the middle of the nineteenth century, which soon became part of the minstrel shows that toured the country. Blacks and whites shared banjo performance into the twentieth century. Europeans brought the violin or fiddle to the New World, where it became established by the late eighteenth century, particularly to accompany dancing. Southern blacks and whites developed a syncopated style that depended on oral transmission and significantly differed from a northern style heavily influenced by Irish musicians and sustained by a print culture. The fiddle-banjo ensemble was also popular in the South. The guitar also migrated from Europe and had developed a musical niche by the early nineteenth century, appearing in concerts and also in middle-class homes, and often played by young women by century's end. It would not become a central folk music instrument until the twentieth century, however.

OTHER ETHNIC GROUPS

In addition to the ballads and musical styles from the British Isles and Africa that seemed to dominate in the nineteenth century, every ethnic group that entered the country brought with it folk songs and dances. Mexicans, with their rich musical heritage, were forcefully incorporated into the United States through the annexation of Texas and the Southwest before the Civil War. Stringed instruments, particularly guitars and violins, and the accordion often accompanied the singing of romances and corridos, both ballad forms. The former, of Spanish origin, was essentially an epic poem and dealt with a tragic or heroic topic, while the latter, originating in the late nineteenth century, usually recounted local events, with the hero demonstrating bravery in overcoming adversity, or describing work experiences. Corridos continue to the present day. Some of the most famous championed the exploits of the accused criminal Gregorio Cortez, and more recently narcocorridos have highlighted narcotics traffickers.

The Irish, arriving in large numbers in northern cities before the Civil War, carried with them traditional ballads and dance tunes. The romantic ballad, such as "The Emigrant's Farewell," expressed a common longing for the loved ones left behind. "Rich Amerikay" also highlighted the pain of emigration, as did many of the ballads. New World hardships were detailed in "No Irish Need Apply" and "Drill, Ye Tarriers, Drill," both of which entered the folk music mainstream. German immigrants, crowding in northern cities by midcentury, introduced singing societies and also expressed longings for the homeland. Some, however, detailed the virtues of coming to a land of democracy and opportunity, such as "Hail to Thee, Columbus, Be Praised." Local taverns were a common site for workers to congregate and sing, with most of the songs coming from Germany.

Because of language barriers, German and other immigrant songs rarely entered the musical mainstream, folk or otherwise. This was true for Scandinavians, Poles, and Italians, for example. Eastern European Jews had a rich musical culture, mostly in Yiddish. Many of the songs expressed various complaints and fears concerning working conditions or family disintegration, or contained religious themes. Broadsides and sheet music of locally composed songs were in wide circulation. While the Yiddish language was limited to Jewish communities, numerous mainstream popular and folk musicians emerged from this rich background in the twentieth century.

Ethnic folk singing societies and festivals also served to promote traditional music and dance. Various German communities in Texas established singing societies in the 1850s, which soon formed into a singers' union and a singing festival in 1853. Such festivals continued into the twentieth century, with traditional German folk songs performed alongside American tunes such as "Oh! Susanna" and "Yellow Rose of Texas." Other ethnic groups in Texas borrowed from German music, including the accordion, polka, and schottische.

Southern Louisiana also proved to be a musical melting pot, combining French Canadian (from Acadia, now known as Nova Scotia), English, Spanish, German, Caribbean, and other styles, resulting in what would be called Cajun (a corruption of Acadian) music and dance. Welsh immigrants in Pennsylvania and Ohio brought with them the traditional eisteddfod, stimulated by the founding of the Welsh National Eisteddfod Association in 1880. In the United States these musical events, often choral competitions, reached an early peak at the Chicago World's Columbian Exposition in 1893, but continued throughout the next century.

By century's end a rich body of ballads, folk songs, spirituals, ethnic songs, instrumental numbers, dance and popular tunes, and much else existed throughout the United States, with regional, racial, and nationality variations. Most folk music functioned as family and community entertainment—for socializing, to be used as cautionary tales, or as messages for social control—generally reflecting local values and aspirations. Much of this vibrant musical life would be part of the broad idea of folk music, if not currently then in the future. But as yet there was little academic interest in studying this rich legacy. That would soon change, as folk music garnered a broad audience and even commercial appeal.

2

1900–1930

Cecil J. Sharp first arrived in the United States from England in 1915 on a tour as the dance advisor for a stage production of *A Midsummer Night's Dream*. Following a talk in Pittsburgh on "English Folk-song," he traveled to Chicago where he met the amateur song collector Olive Dame Campbell. Campbell urged Sharp to visit Appalachia and discover for himself the wealth of folk song and ballad "survivals" around her Asheville, North Carolina home. Intrigued, the following year he returned to the United States and set off on a very productive southern trip that would further strengthen the connection between folk song and ballad collecting in Great Britain and the United States.

Sharp was late to folk music. Born in England in 1859, he obtained a law degree at Cambridge University before moving to Australia in 1882 to practice; he returned to England ten years later determined instead to devote himself to a career in music. While embarking on a period of teaching music and serving as the principal of the Hampstead Conservatory (until 1905), he first heard William Kimber playing the concertina in 1899 and saw the Headington Morris dancers in Oxford. The happenstance experience planted an interest in traditional music. The morris was a traditional dance style seemingly derived from pagan rites, using bells, swords, and sticks to frighten away evil spirits, and usually performed by men.

Four years later Sharp took down the text and tune of "The Seeds of Love" as sung by John England. He was launched on a song collecting career that would last until his death in 1924. With the assistance of the Reverend Charles Marson, Sharp was eventually to collect 1,500 songs in Somerset, a handful of which appeared in the five volumes of *Folk Songs from Somerset* (1904). He had already published *A Book of British Song for Home and School* (1902), soon followed by *English Folk-Song: Some Conclusions* (1907). Sharp didn't trust published song texts, believing that local field collecting would capture the authentic folksongs that had been orally transmitted. He was soon to repudiate his earlier argument in *A Book of British Song for Home and School* that had promoted popular, national songs for the classrooms. Only local vernacular songs, with their musical purity, he insisted, rather than popular tunes should now be taught to students. This was certainly a romantic view, but nonetheless widely shared among the other amateur collectors who gathered in the Folk-Song Society.

Organized in 1898 by Sir Hubert Parry, a director of the Royal College of Music and a professor of Music at Oxford, and other music professionals, the society was designed to promote the circulation of ballads and folk songs in order to promote national unity and moral uplift. This would hopefully counter the perceived rise of class conflict and urban decay, a popular belief of the day among conservatives. The society published the *Journal of the Folk-Song Society*, which included information on English, Irish, and Scottish songs. While the society attracted Ralph Vaughn Williams, Sir Edward Elgar, and other popular composers, it languished until energized by Sharp's involvement after 1904. Sharp stood his ground as a folk song and folk dance purist. He intended to promote nationalism through connecting vernacular music to England's peasant legacy, thereby, he believed, elevating the nation's musical taste and character. Sharp's field collecting and prolific publishing spurred a British folk revival. (Similar folk revivals were taking place in Germany and other European countries.)

Sharp's self-promotion did not go unchallenged—one former colleague complained "He puffed and boomed and shoved and ousted, and used the Press to advertise himself." Moreover, Sharp obtained royalties from folk song and dance books, without compensating the informants. (It was an issue that proved highly charged in Britain and the United States for the next 100 years.) Additionally, composers such as Vaughn Williams, Percy Grainger, and Gustav Holst used folk melodies in their classical compositions (as did many of their European counterparts), and also declined to compensate the traditional performers.

Sharp, despite his large public following, came under criticism from other collectors for his insistence upon musical purity, and he soon preferred to promote traditional dance rather than folk songs. In 1911, he left the Folk-Song Society to head the new English Folk Dance Society; for some years, the promotion of morris dancing was his major commitment. He had already published (with Herbert MacIlwaine) *The Morris Book: A History of Morris Dancing with a Description of Eleven Dances as Performed by the Morris-Men of England* (1907). For all of his interest in the morris dance, he nonetheless issued *One Hundred English Folksongs* in 1916. In the introduction to that collection he noted: "The careful preservation of its folk-music is to a nation a matter of the highest import…. The collection and preservation of our folk-music, whatever else it had done, has at least restored the Englishman's confidence in the inherent ability of his nation to produce great music."

When Sharp arrived in the United States he was *the* recognized authority on English folk song and traditional dance, convinced that because the United States lacked a feudal peasantry it possessed no true folk music. Olive Dame Campbell would soon convince him otherwise. Campbell, originally from Massachusetts and living in North Carolina, was married to John Campbell, a field worker for the philanthropic Russell Sage Foundation. As the Campbells traveled throughout the Appalachian region, while John investigated school conditions, his wife began collecting mountain ballads. By 1910 she had assembled songs and ballads from singers in Kentucky, Georgia, and Tennessee, but could not find a publisher. Native white folk songs had been overlooked in the nineteenth century, but this soon changed when W. W. Newell, a Harvard professor and founder of the American Folklore Society, published two articles on "Early American Ballads" at century's end in the *Journal of American Folklore* (*JAF*).

Campbell was not the only person to recognize the importance of the folk songs all about her. Katherine Pettit and May Stone, the founders of the Hindman Settlement School in Knott County, Kentucky, in 1902, collected local ballads from children at the school. Pettit submitted musical samples to Harvard professor George Lyman Kittredge, Child's protégé and successor, who published them as "Ballads and Rhymes from Kentucky" in the *JAF* in 1907. Similarly, Hubert Shearin and Josiah Combs's *A Syllabus of Kentucky Folk-Songs* (1911) included 20 Child ballads out of 333 published songs. E. C. Perrow followed with almost 300 "Songs and Rhymes from the South" in the *JAF* in 1912–1915, drawn from both white and black singers in Tennessee, Kentucky, Mississippi, Missouri, West Virginia, and Alabama.

Josephine McGill, who lived in Louisville, published *Folk-Songs of the Kentucky Mountains* in 1917. "From another ancient dame we heard 'Lord Randal' and 'The

CECIL SHARP

Cecil Sharp was born in London in 1859. After obtaining his law degree at Cambridge University, he moved to Australia in 1882, where he initially practiced law and also worked in a bank. But he was more interested in his music studies, and he became an assistant organist at the Adelaide Cathedral and director of the school of music there. Upon returning to England in 1892 he taught music at the Ludgrove School and became the principal of the Hampstead Conservatory, as well as beginning his publications with *British Songs for Home and School* (1902). He now devoted his attention to collecting and promoting the study and preservation of English folk songs and dances, with the longtime assistance of Maud Karpeles (1885–1976). In his field collecting he was among the first to write down both a song's words and tune. Perhaps his most significant contribution was the establishment of the English Folk Dance Society in 1911, and he directed a School of Folk Song and Dance at Stratford-upon-Avon. During World War I he twice traveled to the United States with Karpeles, in order to collect folk songs in a few southern States, some of which first appeared in their book *English Folk Songs of the Southern Appalachians* (1917).

Sharp argued that "traditional" English folk songs and dances captured a lost rural world, which had been disappearing because of the encroachments of modern society. While his ideas were controversial, he gained wide recognition for his zeal in promoting folk music and dance. His numerous publications included *Folk Songs from Somerset* (1904–1909), *The Morris Book* (1907–1913), *Country Dance Tunes* (1909–1922), *The Sword Dances of Northern England* (1911–1913), *English Folk Carols* (1911), *English Folk Chanteys* (1914), *One Hundred English Folk-Songs* (1916), and *Folk-Songs of English Origin* (1921–1923), among others. He died in 1924. Six years later the Cecil Sharp House opened in London, headquarters of the Folk Dance Society, which today remains as the home of the English Folk Dance and Song Society. With the assistance of A. H. Fox Strangways, Karpeles published the biography *Cecil Sharp* in 1933.

Gypsy Laddie,' sung in a squalid mountain cabin to tunes of much charm," McGill wrote. New Yorkers Loraine Wyman and Howard Brockway visited Hindman and the nearby Pine Mountain Settlement School (founded in 1913) in 1916 to gather songs. Traveling throughout much of Kentucky, they quickly published *Lonesome Tunes: Folksongs of the Kentucky Mountain*, which included numerous ballads published earlier by Child. They focused on what they considered traditional ballads and folk songs, with British origins (although changed over the years, often becoming less violent), believing (erroneously) that mountain folk were luckily untouched by modern society, therefore pure and simple. In fact, most southerners' lives were influenced by the growing industrialization of the region and modern communications, and they were hardly culturally isolated.

When Sharp learned of Olive Dame Campbell's southern ballad collection, he changed his mind about collecting possibilities in the United States. He also felt competition from Wyman, Brockway, and other active collectors. So, accompanied by his assistant, Maud Karpeles, Sharp arrived in Asheville in July 1916. Guided by Campbell, they immediately set off to find traditional singers, eventually to collect 400 songs from 67 singers in North Carolina, Tennessee, and Virginia.

Focusing on Child ballads and "traditional" folk songs, Sharp ignored religious music, popular and topical tunes, instrumental songs, and urban/industrial areas. From this first trip and Olive Dame Campbell's previous work they published *English Folk Songs of the Southern Appalachians* in 1917, a work that included 40 Child ballads, two dozen additional English ballads, and more than 70 local songs and nursery songs. The work was a success. "I am so glad of your genuine appreciation of the mountain people," John Campbell wrote to Sharp in late 1916, "for I grow weary of the many who come to the mountains simply to exploit the mountaineer."

After a short stay in England, Sharp and Karpeles returned to Tennessee, Kentucky, and North Carolina in 1917 and collected another 600 songs from white singers. Despite continuing ill health, Sharp managed to visit Virginia and North Carolina in April 1918, ending with another 625 tunes before returning to England. He presided over the expansion of the English Folk Dance Society, offering classes in London that attracted a weekly attendance of 1,000. Until his death in 1924, Sharp continued to believe that only ballads, folk songs, and dances seemingly untainted by modern society should be collected and promoted.

During the 1920s, with the passing of such pioneer collectors as Sharp, Lucy Broadwood, Frank Kidson, and Cecil Baring-Gould, the Folk-Song Society fell on hard times, and there were few important scholarly collections published. Beginning in 1921 Ernest John Moeran recorded the traditional East Norfolk singer and farmer Harry Cox, as well as his neighbors, often in local pubs on Saturday nights. Cox was eventually to sing more than 100 songs, most of which he had learned through oral tradition. Alfred Williams, one of the few collectors born in a working-class family, published *Songs of the Upper Thames* in 1923. But to the romantics of the first generation, the well was running dry. In 1931 Vaughan Williams pessimistically commented that "the materials for publication is now practically exhausted and it is most unlikely that any new material will be discovered." With only 123 members in 1933, the Folk-Song Society merged with the much larger (almost 2,000 members) English Folk Dance Society, creating the English Folk Dance and Song Society (EFDSS).

Before his death in 1924, Sharp was unable to publish an expanded edition of his southern collections, but Maud Karpeles finally issued *English Folk Songs from the Southern Appalachians* in 1932 containing 274 songs in 968 variations, as well as a few play-party games. Among the songs are scattered American ballads such as "John Hardy," "Poor Omie," and "The Lonesome Prairie." Folklorist David Whisnant has concluded that despite Sharp's traditional values and romantic view of rural southerners, "he was by all odds the best-trained, most humane and open-minded collector working in the area at the time." While certainly not definitive, his southern collection set a high standard. As for Olive Dame Campbell, she founded the John C. Campbell Folk School near Brasstown, North Carolina, in 1925 and remained active in promoting traditional southern arts and crafts until her death in 1954. Sharp and Campbell together demonstrated the close connection between ballad collectors and folk music in England and the United States, which would long continue.

COWBOY SONGS

While Sharp, Campbell, and a growing number of others were scouring the southern backwoods for examples of British and native American songs, John Lomax had begun exploring western cowboy music. Born in 1867, Lomax grew up in frontier Texas, graduated from the University of Texas in 1897, and in 1906 entered the English graduate program at Harvard University. Lomax studied with George Lyman Kittredge, Barrett Wendell, and other pioneers in promoting the study of ballads and Medieval English literature, as well as American literature and folk music. Kittredge and Wendell especially encouraged him to begin collecting the cowboy ballads and songs of Lomax's native west. He mostly solicited songs and ballads through newspaper notices, rather than doing much field work, and copied old songsters.

Lomax's *Cowboy Songs and Other Frontier Ballads* appeared in 1910. At the same time southern collectors were searching for, and discovering, indications of surviving English and Scottish ballads, particularly those published by Francis Child. Lomax, however, with the encouragement of Child's colleague Kittredge, sought out uniquely western folk songs. Yet Lomax could not discount their historic ties, and, he believed, the romantic, primitive circumstances that gave rise to the songs. "Illiterate people, and people cut off from newspapers and books, isolated and lonely—thrown back on primal resources for entertainment and for the expression of emotion—utter themselves through some-what the same character of songs as did their forefathers of perhaps a thousand years ago," Lomax explained in his introduction. "The songs represent the operation of instinct and tradition." He was interested in occupational songs, not the traditional Anglo-American ballads. *Cowboy Songs* included "The Buffalo Skinners," "Old Paint," "Sweet Betsy From Pike," and the recently composed "Home On the Range." In 1920 he published a brief sequel, *Songs of the Cattle Trail and Cow Camp* (and in 1938, along with his son Alan, he issued an expanded version of *Cowboy Songs*). After the original *Cowboy Songs* appeared, Lomax gave a series of talks on college campuses, and he realized "that our native folk songs awakened interest among intelligent people," as he later noted in his 1947 autobiography, *Adventures of a Ballad Hunter*.

Cowboys, real and imagined, had been celebrated in dime novels and in Wild West shows since the Civil War, but it only became apparent that those "illiterate" cowboys were writing songs as early as in the 1890s. D. J. O'Malley wrote "When the Work's All Done This Fall" in 1893; it would later become the first popular cowboy recording when released by Carl T. Sprague in 1925. Jack Thorp composed "Little Joe, the Wrangler" five years later, and he issued *Songs of the Cowboy* in 1908, two years before Lomax's book.

Cowboys probably did often sing to quiet the herds at night, fitting new words to old folk songs and ballads, but not until the publication of the Thorp and Lomax books

JOHN LOMAX

John Avery Lomax was born in Mississippi in 1875, but soon moved to Texas, his home for the rest of his life. He began to collect cowboy songs as a teenager, but abandoned his search when he enrolled at the University of Texas in the mid-1890s. After graduation he moved around a bit, then entered Harvard where he studied folklore with George Lyman Kittredge and renewed his interest in western songs, leading to publication of *Cowboy Songs and Other Frontier Ballads in* 1910, a pioneering, influential collection of American songs. For Lomax's biographer Nolan Porterfield, "The ultimate value of *Cowboy Songs* is measured not in scholarly abstractions but in what it gave us all, in those lovely, sad, and funny bits of tune and line now embedded in our lives: "Whoopee Ti Yi Yo, Git Along, Little Dogies," "The Old Chisholm Trail," "Jesse James," "Sweet Betsy from Pike," and of course, "Home on the Range." He tried a variety of occupations, including teaching at Texas A&M College and serving as Secretary of the University of Texas, and even tried his hand in the banking business. But he returned to his folk music passion in 1933, with a collecting trip through the South with his son Alan, the first of many that would produce hundreds of recordings.

John and Alan Lomax published *American Ballads and Folk Songs* in 1934, a rich compilation heavily drawn from their field trips. They divided the ballads and songs into various categories, such as railroad and levee camp songs, white desperadoes, cocaine and whisky, the blues, and much more. John was now the "Honorary Consultant in American Folk Song and Curator of the Song Archives of the Library of Congress," which gave him access to the library's recording equipment and an official identity as he continued his southern collecting and publishing. He issued *Negro Songs As Sung by Lead Belly* in 1936 and *Our Singing Country: A Second Volume of American Ballads and Folk Songs* in 1941 also with Alan. Lomax published his autobiography, *Adventures of a Ballad Hunter*, in 1947 the year before his death. A pioneering field collector, he left an impressive legacy of recordings in the Library of Congress that have remained invaluable; although he is perhaps best remembered as the one who discovered the brilliant songster Lead Belly in prison in Louisiana and initiated his remarkable public career.

were the songs more widely known. (Dr. Brewster Higley, the author of "Home On the Range" in 1873, was no cowboy, but his art song was soon considered a folk song.) Charles Siringo issued *The Song Companion of a Lone Star Cowboy* in 1919, while Charles Finger first published *Sailor Chantey's and Cowboy Songs* in 1923. Typewriter salesman Bentley Ball had the first commercial cowboy recordings in 1919, "Jesse James" and "The Dying Cowboy"; he was soon followed by Carl Sprague and Vernon Dalhart. While there was little musical or textual connection between cowboy songs and southern mountain tunes, the two would later be lumped together under the commercial designation Country and Western music.

COUNTRY GOES COMMERCIAL

As the ballad and folk song collectors were continually discovering, throughout the country, not just in the South, there was no lack of people singing and playing in their homes and communities. Ballads and folk songs were common among the folk. With the developing mass media, however, particularly phonograph records after the turn of the century, and radio following World War I, folk music was becoming increasingly commercial and widespread. Almost simultaneously, southern rural performers were heard over the airwaves and on records.

Old-time fiddlers A. C. "Eck" Robertson, from Texas, and Henry Gilliland, from Oklahoma, traveled uninvited to New York City on July 1, 1922, and were able to record the tunes "Sally Gooden" and "Arkansas Traveler" at the Victor Records studio. This is considered the first commercial country record. Fiddlin' John Carson followed in June 1923, when Ralph Peer, who worked for Okeh records, traveled to Atlanta, Georgia, to record the champion fiddler at the urging of furniture store owner Polk Brockman. Carson's "The Little Old Log Cabin in the Lane" and "The Old Hen Cackled and the Rooster's Going to Crow" unexpectedly became the first country music hits. Soon after multi-instrumentalist and singer Henry Whitter released "Lonesome Road Blues" and "Wreck on the Southern Old 97." Numerous record companies—Brunswick, Gennett, Paramount, Victor, and Columbia, as well as Okeh—had discovered a musical gold mine in "old familiar tunes" and "old-time music" (often characterized as "hillbilly" songs after 1925).

Individual performers, string bands, duos and trios, and various combinations were soon crowding around recording horns set up in recording studios, hotel rooms, or anywhere else where the sounds could be captured. "The early hillbilly musicians, for the most part, were folk performers who stood in transition between the traditional milieu that had nourished them and the larger popular arena which beckoned," Bill Malone, the music's prime historian, has written. "Folk musicians did not cease to be folk merely because they stepped in front of a recording or radio microphone, nor did the original audience change instantaneously. But once a career began to blossom and the audience began to expand through radio coverage, record sales, and the like, the temptation to alter a style or freshen one's repertory might become resistible."

But most important, Malone notes, the "early commercial performers were, by and large, working people who played music in their leisure hours." One notable exception was Vernon Dalhart, a professional singer with a trained voice, who recorded extensively through the decade under a variety of pseudonyms. His hits included "The Wreck of the Old 97" and "The Prisoner's Song."

Other important performers included Charlie Poole and the North Carolina Ramblers, the Skillet Lickers (groups often had deliberately hokey names), Bradley Kincaid, Buell Kazee, Kelly Harrell, and Ernest Stoneman. Their songs were either selected from a broad nineteenth century folk and popular legacy, or were recently composed songs and ballads. Carson Robison, for example, wrote numerous fresh hillbilly tunes such as "Wreck of the Number Nine" and "Carry Me Back to the Lone Prairie." Event songs, often about real tragedies, were widespread, such as Andrew "Blind Andy" Jenkins's very popular "The Death of Floyd Collins."

Oddly, the two most influential and popular performing acts were discovered during the same recording session in Bristol, Tennessee, in late July/early August 1927. Ralph Peer, using a then state-of-the-art electronic recording system, recorded a number of performers over nine days, including the previously recorded Ernest "Pop" Stoneman, Blind Alfred Reed, Uncle Eck Dunford playing "Skip to Ma Lou," the first recording of this common play-party song, and most significantly Jimmie Rodgers and the Carter Family. A. P. Carter, his wife Sara, and her cousin (and A. P.'s sister-in-law) Maybelle, were from Scott County, Virginia, and had a broad repertoire of traditional ballads and sacred songs. They would eventually record more than 300 sides for various companies, including the enduring "Wildwood Flower," "The Wabash Cannonball," "Little Darling, Pal of Mine," "Worried Man Blues," and "Will the Circle Be Unbroken." They would enjoy a long, highly influential career.

On the same day Peer recorded Rodgers, a former railroad man from Mississippi, who had a unique voice and presentation. Until his untimely death from tuberculosis in 1933, Rodgers was a transforming figure, the first country singing star, a singer and songwriter who revolutionized the developing profession. He introduced the blue yodel, combining both black and white influences, with such songs as "T for Texas," and also made hits out of "Away Out on the Mountain," "TB Blues," and "Peach Picking Time in Georgia." (Numerous others began their careers as Rodgers's musical clones, including the later cowboy star Gene Autry.)

Musicians developed professional lives through recordings and personal appearances, and especially with their performances on the proliferating number of country radio shows. Commercial radio was launched in Pittsburgh in 1920, and two years later Fiddlin' John Carson appeared on an Atlanta station. The launching of the *Barn Dance* on WLS in Chicago in 1924, however, began the era of regular country music shows. Over the years the *Barn Dance* promoted the careers of many musicians, beginning with Bradley Kincaid. More well known, and still going into the twenty-first century, was Nashville's *Grand Ole' Opry* (originally the *WSM Barn Dance*) begun in 1925 by George Hay. Early performers included Dr. Humphrey Bate and the Possum Hunters, The Fruit Jar Drinkers, the Gully Jumpers (Hay liked folksy-sounding names), Sam and Kirk McGee, and particularly Uncle Dave Macon, a rollicking banjo player. While performers were hardly paid for their radio appearances, these spots became vital for promoting their record sales and concert appearances. Radio barn dance shows would proliferate throughout the country in the 1930s. The only black radio performer was harmonica whiz DeFord Bailey on the *Grand Ole Opry*, starring from 1926 to 1941 (his race was not identified for the listening audience).

AFRICAN-AMERICAN INFLUENCES

With some exceptions, white academic collectors were not particularly interested in black music early in the twentieth century. Southern sociologist Howard Odum published 100 African-American religious songs in the *American Journal of Religious Psychology and Education* in 1906, followed with 115 secular songs in *JAF* in 1911. Henry C. Davis printed a similar collection in *JAF* in 1914, and E. C. Perrow included black "Songs and Rhymes from the South" at the same time in *JAF*. Most published sources focused on older spirituals, such as John W. Work and his brother Frederick J. Work in their booklet *Folk Songs of American Negro* in 1907. They wrote: "Still away down in the Negro's heart there has been a smouldering coal of love for his own peculiar songs which have been gradually fanned into a burning flame by two forces, education and knowledge that musicians of other people are studying it seriously."

John Work, James Weldon Johnson, Nathaniel Dett, and other African-American composers collected spirituals and arranged them into a modern classical format, mostly to be used in church services. Trained choirs became more common, particularly in black Pentacostal churches. At the same time, commercial phonograph records began appearing as early as the Kentucky Jubilee Singers recording in 1894. The Fisk Jubilee Singers were brought to the Victor Talking Machine Company studio in New Jersey in 1909 by John Work. They first performed "Swing Low, Sweet Chariot," "Roll, Jordan, Roll," and even Stephen Foster's "Old Black Joe." The Jubilees issued records for the next two decades. The Tuskegee Institute Singers were much less prolific, recording for Victor only in 1914 and 1915. Meanwhile, from 1910 to 1918 a Colored Music Festival in Atlanta featured spirituals, known as "Plantation Melodies," that attracted both whites and blacks.

The blues was considered the secular counter to spirituals, the developing gospel style, and other church-related music. Defining the "blues" is virtually impossible, so that Elijah Wald, in 2004, in his very informative *Escaping the Delta: Robert Johnson and the Invention of the Blues*, believes "that if a black person played it before 1950, and it is not classifiable as jazz, classical or gospel, then it must be blues." He also remarks that before the 1960s the blues was "Whatever the mass of black record buyers called 'blues' in any period." As the blues developed, however, there was also a significant connection between black and white performers, so that racial distinctions have not been particularly evident in songs and performances. A blues style seemed to emerge sometime in the late nineteenth century, principally in the Mississippi Delta region, according to most accounts.

W. C. Handy, a professional band leader, published "The Memphis Blues (Mr. Crump)" in 1912, the same year that "Dallas Blues" and "Baby Seals Blues" appeared in sheet music. "Memphis Blues" was recorded in 1914 by the Victor Military Band, sounding more like a ragtime march than a blues tune; ragtime songs were then very popular. The next year Morton Harvey, a white performer, recorded "Memphis Blues," and for the next few years other white singers recorded folk-style blues, including Nora Bayes. The first black "blues" singer, Mamie Smith, did not enter a studio until 1920. Moreover, Wald argues, her hit record, "Crazy Blues," sounded more like a Tin Pan Alley torch song than a rural blues tune. "This is not to say that it was less genuine blues than the folkier songs," he notes, "but only to reemphasize the fact that such categories are infinitely mutable, arbitrary divisions of a continuum." Musical classifications—blues, country, jazz, bluegrass, gospel, spirituals, folk, classical, etc.—are not absolute, but always relative and flexible.

BLUES

By the 1920s the blues had been developing in various parts of the South, with similarities as well as differences in style and words based on local conditions as well as commercial influences. Rural performers in the Mississippi Delta, for example, with its very large black population, contained aspects of older African melodies and instrumental styles. Texas produced a somewhat different sound, as was true in the Southeast. According to the blues scholar Samuel Charters, the blues developed out of "the singing of the West African griots, the holler, the work song, [and] the song traditions of the southern countryside." The recording of blues performers accelerated after 1920, first featuring Gertrude "Ma" Rainey, Bessie Smith, Ida Cox, Sara Martin, and other female classic blues performers. The female classic blues singers performed in theaters with a jazz band, had elaborate costumes and settings, and often sang their own compositions. The male blues singers, however, were usually alone or in a small group, played acoustic instruments, particularly the guitar and piano, and appeared in juke joints and other local places. The blues queens were usually more popular than the male singers, such as Sylvester Weaver, Papa Charlie Jackson, Lonnie Johnson, and particularly Blind Lemon Jefferson from Texas, who were recorded starting in mid-decade. Charley Patton, Mississippi John Hurt, as well as the Memphis Jug Band and Cannon's Jug Stompers, were turning out records by the end of the decade, but Bessie Smith remained "Empress of the Blues."

Should these blues performers be considered doing folk or popular music? The answer is not clear. While the male singer–guitar players appeared to be performing traditional songs, they were certainly exposed to the commercial music of the time. Indeed, the Florida-Georgia guitar player Blind Blake performed numerous blues numbers, but he also recorded ragtime and minstrel tunes. Blind Willie McTell and Peg Leg Howell performed ragtime, hillbilly, minstrel, and gospel as well as the blues. Elijah Wald, in *Escaping the Delta*, has argued that these and other rural performers should be considered professional musicians who absorbed and performed a wide range of music. That is, "rural black Delta dwellers were not only aware of all sorts of nonblues, non-Mississippi music, but were doing their best to keep up with the latest developments." This was true throughout the South, among blacks and whites alike. By the late 1920s piano players such as Leroy Carr, who lived in Indianapolis, and the Chicago-based duo of Tampa Red (Hudson Whitaker) and Georgia Tom (Thomas A. Dorsey), were definitely professionals. Some performers were incredibly popular, with Tampa Red recording 251 sides between 1928 and 1942, Big Bill Broonzy 224 sides, Lonnie Johnson 191 sides, and Bessie Smith farther down the list with 160 sides between 1923 and 1933. Wald continues, "These were the stars, the popular professionals who had the hits that the rural players learned, imitated, and reworked for local fans. They are not the whole story of the blues era, but they were by far the most visible and influential figures, and the ones who defined the style for the vast majority of its audience." He goes on to comment, however, that "plenty of people did play blues at home to relax after a day's work . . . and this kind of informal music making was far more common before phonographs, radio, and television made professional entertainment accessible in every living room." This trend had started earlier in the century when the phonograph had begun to replace the piano as the main source of music in most homes throughout the country.

While record company executives and their agents were searching the South for "traditional" musicians to record, there was an increasing scholarly interest in African-American music. In 1925, Dorothy Scarborough in *On the Trail of Negro Folk-Songs* divided her lengthy book into various topics: folk songs, ballads, dance songs, children's game songs, lullabies, songs about animals, work songs, railroad songs, and a short last chapter on the blues. For her understanding of the latter she depended on W. C. Handy and was not interested in the current outpouring of blues recordings. "Each town has its local blues," she notes, "no aspect of life being without its expression in song." But she preferred work songs and ballads, seemingly more authentic. Howard Odum and Guy Johnson's *The Negro and His Songs*, published in 1925, has a similar division (religious songs, social songs, and work songs), but with no designation for the blues. Odum began collecting in Georgia and Mississippi in 1905, leading to his pioneering 1909 Ph.D. dissertation in psychology at Clark University, which his biographer describes as "the first collection of American folk song to deal systematically and sympathetically with black secular music." Parts soon appeared in two articles about "Folk-song and Folk-poetry: As Found in the Secular Songs of the Southern Negroes," and later in his book with Johnson. Enlightened white southerners, Odum and Johnson professed not to make judgments, but their rather romantic views led them to conclude that "the processes of civilization are operating to make the Negro ashamed of his old spirituals and to relegate the more naïve of his social songs to a rapidly diminishing lower class. Slowly but surely the folk creative urge will be dulled and this great body of folk song, perhaps the last of its kind, will surely pass away." In 1926 they published *Negro Workday Songs*, including a long section on blues songs, which they now believed are "probably the Negro's most distinctive contribution to American art."

In *American Negro Folk-Songs* published in 1928, Newman White approached his study as an academic, yet was also influenced by the predominate racism of the day. In a short chapter on "Race-Consciousness," he notes that "the Negro laborer is sometimes surly; of course, he sometimes growls and is dissatisfied with his lot. But the real significance of his songs expressing race-consciousness is the fact that they show so little of this mood. Fundamentally, they are striking evidence of the deep conservatism, humor, patience, and sense of present realities with which the Negro has contributed probably more than his full share to the concord of the two races in the South." Most collectors, but not all, shared White's optimistic views. The reality was just the opposite, however, that racial segregation and discrimination, supported by law and enforced through public and private intimidation and violence, was widespread throughout the South. As for the blues, White had little to say: "Most blues sung by Negroes today have only a secondary folk origin; their primary source is the phonograph record"; and perhaps for this reason, he concluded: "The vogue of the blues is already on the wane, but their influence on Negro folk-song is only in its first stage."

The role of the blues in individual lives can perhaps be understood through the experiences of David Honeyboy Edwards, who would become a professional blues musician. Born in the Delta, in 1929 he was 14 years old and experienced the blues in various ways. He obtained a guitar, a second-hand Sears Roebuck Stella that was sold to his father for eight dollars. Taught by his father, he was soon playing for local parties, having learned "John Henry" and "Joe Turner Blues." At the same time the family obtained a record player, and his sister continually played a Blind Lemon Jefferson record. He also heard Tommy McClennan, Tommy Johnson, and Sonny Boy Williamson (aka Rice Miller) performing locally. These were the blues sources and influences that were available in the Delta (and throughout much of the South), a combination of commercial culture and local possibilities.

FOLK BECOMES MORE ACADEMIC AND POPULAR

In 1925, the Harvard University Press published John Harrington Cox's *Folk-Songs of the South,* collected with the cooperation of the West Virginia Folk-Lore Society and dedicated to George Lyman Kittredge. The previous year Harvard had issued Roland Gray's *Songs and Ballads of the Maine Lumberjacks,* indicating an interest beyond the South. Cox met many traditional singers, white and black, including one old woman who "made her living ... by washing, begging, and selling off things that she could get along without. Times were hard, men were out of work, and women were doing their own washing instead of sending it out." She sang "Jesse James" and "Johnny Collins," "in a low contralto voice, heavy and mournful." Cox began with numerous variations of Child ballads, starting with "Lady

Isabel and the Elf Knight," but also included "John Hardy," "Davy Crockett," "Putting On the Style," "The Arkansaw Traveller," and other local standards. Cox noted not only his informant for each song, but also where the lyrics might have previously been published. While D. K. Wilgus later had both praise and criticism for Cox's methodology, he did indicate that he set the "standard for most editors with any sort of academic interest in folk song. The regional archivists and the lone academics naturally followed Cox's lead, their aim being to present their collected materials fully and accurately, to be approved and studied by other academics." The almost invisible line between folk and popular songs was evident in Henry Schoemaker's *North Pennsylvania Minstrelsy* (1919). He included not only older folk songs and ballads, and newer songs from the state's lumber camps, but also compositions such as Stephen Foster's "Oh! Susanna!"

While Cox and others were presenting folk songs and ballads in an academic setting to a limited audience, Carl Sandburg successfully tapped into the growing popular market. The award winning poet and historian published *The American Songbag* (1927), which has always remained in print. "There is presented herein a collection of 280 songs, ballads, ditties, brought together from all regions of America," he explained in the introduction. "The music includes not merely airs and melodies, but complete harmonization or piano accompaniments. It is an all-American affair, marshaling the genius of thousands of original singing Americans." Sandburg's collection was designed to be studied as well as performed. While he recognized the importance of the academic publications, he admitted that he also personally collected many of the selections. The ballads and songs were divided into various categories: dramas and portraits, minstrel songs, pioneer memories, prison and jail songs, Mexican border songs, railroad and work gangs, and much more. "Ballad singers of centuries ago and mule-

skinners alive and singing today helped make this book,"
Sandburg explained. "Pioneers, pick and shovel men, team-
sters, mountaineers, and people often called ignorant have
their hands and voices in this book, along with minstrels,
sophisticates, and trained musicians." His expansive democratic politics guided his musical approach and broad out-
reach. While records and radio shows were now widely
available, replacing the parlor piano as the center of musical
life in an increasing number of homes, Sandburg counted
on the continuing popularity of homemade performance.
And he was not wrong.

Folk songs differed somewhat in various sections of the
country, demonstrating the role of economic, geographical, ethnic, nationality, and racial diversity since the seventeenth century. For example, Child ballads were rather
common in New England, as well as songs about farming,
whaling, sailing, and work in the timber and textile industries. Also common were songs from the Revolutionary War
and War of 1812, which were rare in other sections. Child
ballads also circulated widely in the Southeast, along with
broadside ballads such as "Pretty Polly" and "Jack Monroe." Murder ballads had more of a local nature, along with
mine and train disaster tunes. In the deep South songs from
the African-American tradition, such as "John Henry,"
"Stagolee," and "Boll Weevil" circulated widely. Throughout the Midwest and Great Lakes region the presence of
Scandinavian and German immigrants meant songs from
their homelands, as well as ballads about lumbering, such
as "The Jam on Gerry's Rocks," and sailing. The "Little Old
Sod Shanty on My Claim" expressed the unique experience
of trying to carve out a farm on the Great Plains, while
"The Dreary Black Hills" is probably self-explanatory. The
Far West encompassed songs from the other regions, as well
as the experiences from gold and hard-rock mining, cattle
ranching, railroading, lumbering, and other work places.
Texas produced "The Yellow Rose of Texas," "The Texas

Ranger," and so many others. "Sweet Betsy from Pike,"
"The Buffalo Skinners," "Ho for California," and "Streets
of Laredo" certainly captured life on the western frontier.
Americans had not only a common song heritage, but also
rich musical regional diversity that would come together
in the twentieth century. "In antebellum [before the Civil
War] America, regional cultures were very distinct even
though their origins were somewhat complicated," Norm
Cohen has explained in *Folk Music: A Regional Exploration* (2005). "Later, other more efficient means of passing a
song from one person to the next gradually began the process of blurring regional cultural boundaries." Still, after
such a long process of seeming homogenization, regional,
as well as ethnic and racial variations, continued to exist
into the twenty-first century. The North and the white
South differed greatly, for example, concerning what songs
from the Civil War would be recalled and performed.

THE ROLE OF THE FEDERAL GOVERNMENT

An increasing number of individuals were searching the
country, far and wide, for folk songs and ballads, and publishing their rich findings. For example, Phillips Barry's
British Ballads from Maine, George Korson's *Songs and
Ballads of the Anthracite Miner*, Franz Rickaby's *Ballads and Songs of the Shanty-Boy*, Joanna Colcord's *Roll
and Go: Songs of American Sailormen*, Fannie Hardy
Eckstorm and Mary Winslow Smyth's *Minstrelsy of
Maine*, and Arthur Davis's *Traditional Ballads of Virginia*. The Schirmer company published a number of
intriguing songbooks, for example *Bayou Ballads, Seven
Negro Exaltations* and *Spanish Songs of Old California*.

Field collectors were cautious in selecting who to inter-
view and what songs and ballads to focus on. There were, for
example, differences between the musical experiences and
memories of men and women. Jennifer Post has recently

made these distinctions in her study of traditional music in northern New England: "While women (and their music) dominated the kitchen during the daytime, men controlled the music performed there on a Saturday night, when families gathered for the local kitchen dances or men met for jam sessions. The parlor, on the other hand, was often used by men to relax in the evening and to share songs with their children, yet it was used by women in the afternoons for local work bees and other social gatherings where they sometimes sang songs and hymns." Men mostly performed in public, women in private. And the songs they recalled varied in form and content, although often collectors did not register such differences. Another problem for collectors concerned songs with bawdy or salacious themes and words. Collectors often preferred to overlook such tunes, and publishers certainly refused to print any songs considered offensive. "The prudery that prevented erotic folklore from being collected or published in the first pace, in the English-speaking world, has left a certain residual fuzziness as to why it is worth collecting and studying now," Gershon Legman has written in his introduction to Vance Randolph's *Roll Me in Your Arms: "Unprintable" Ozark Folksongs and Folklore* (1992). Randolph (1892–1980) moved to Missouri in 1920 and soon began his study of local folklore. He published *Ozark Mountain Folks* in 1932, and other studies quickly followed, culminating in the four volumes of *Ozark Folksongs* (1946–1950), but without any of the bawdy materials that he had picked up in his travels. "I made no special effort to collect lewd songs," Randolph explained, "but my informants sang them anyhow, and I recorded bawdy pieces along with the other items." Other collectors were much more cautious, and usually avoided such songs altogether.

Despite the selective nature of much collecting, the country overflowed with traditional songs and ballads. It appeared time for the federal government to get involved.

On July 1, 1928, the Library of Congress established the Archive of American Folk-Song. Carl Engel, chief of the Library's Music Division, appointed Robert Winslow Gordon as the collection's first director. Previously a student of Harvard's George Lyman Kittredge, Gordon had taught briefly in the University of California's English department, but preferred to hang around the San Francisco waterfront. There he collected folk songs from the local denizens and hobos, which fueled his monthly "Old Songs That Men Have Sung" column in *Adventure* magazine (1923–1928). In 1925 he began collecting folk songs in North Carolina, and soon after in Georgia, before accepting the position in Washington. He published his findings in a series of 15 essays in *The New York Times Sunday Magazine* (1927–1928), which later appeared in his book *Folk-Songs of America*. Gordon lasted in the Archive until 1933. An erratic administrator, he yet established a basis for the collection of publications, field recordings, and films that would mushroom over the decades.

DECADE ENDS

Folk-style ballads and folk songs—ethnic, blues, hillbilly, traditional, shanties, cowboy, and the like—could not compete with popular songs from Tin Pan Alley or the upsurge of (black and white) jazz for the attention of the general public and a large share of the mass media. Yet there was always a local interest and commercial market for such sounds, connecting past with present, but often in complex ways. Both mainstream and small labels issued numerous ethnic records, marketing to an audience eager to connect with the Old World. Victor Green has noted that "Recorded ethnic music was not the only cultural accomplishment of immigrant Americans during the 1920s; the decade was also an era, in fact a golden age, of onstage immigrant entertainment," often including songs. The major labels—

Victor, Edison, Columbia—released records for the ethnic market of Poles, Finns, Swedes, Irish, Germans, Ukrainians, and others. Columbia had a specialty ethnic series by 1928, and Victor soon followed, now including immigrants from Albania, India, China, and Jews from Eastern Europe who preferred klezmer music. There were also numerous smaller labels with an ethnic focus, such as Banner, Gennett, and Brunswick. Early radio programs also might feature ethnic performers, for example in the Upper Midwest. Radio stations in the Minneapolis–St. Paul area, started in the 1920s with programs combining "ethnic Old Time with Country Music," as James Leary has written.

The musical influence of Henry Ford, the genius behind mass automobile manufacturing and sales, was noteworthy. While Ford promoted social and technological change, he simultaneously longed for a lost, familiar, simpler, rural world. Ford sponsored a book of old-time dance steps, welcomed traditional musicians to his headquarters in Dearborn, Michigan, and had square dancing classes in the Ford Motor Company ballroom. Ford car dealers sponsored fiddle contests throughout the country, topped by a national championship in 1926, won by a southerner, Uncle Bunt Stephens, who collected $1,000. Maine champion fiddler Millie Dunham used his trip to Dearborn to launch a national vaudeville tour for a few years, mixing musical nostalgia with commercial appeal. Dunham's career captured the complexities not only of Ford's backward look and revolutionary business skills, but also of the larger world of contemporary folk music. It both pointed to the past and headed into a commercial future.

The 1920s ended not with a bang but with a whimper. The stock market crashed in late 1929, setting off a worldwide depression that would last for another decade. Folk music would not, could not, fade away, however, as it became increasingly commercial as well as widespread in both Britain and the United States. It would take on somewhat new forms, particularly as it was picked up by those in the Communist Party and others on the Left and increasingly connected with labor unions. Collectors would continue to collect and publish their findings, radio shows would proliferate, record companies would drastically cut back their offerings, and music festivals would flourish. In the United States, more than in Britain, the federal government would become particularly involved, as the people's folk culture, past and present, took on new meaning and importance. In both countries folk music would take on fresh dimensions.

3

1930–1950

GREAT BRITAIN

Cecil Sharp's legacy stretched long after his death in 1924. Traditional songs and dances were promoted by the English Folk Dance and Song Society (EFDSS), carrying forward a commitment to the belief that folk songs were rooted in a distant past and could preserve a distinctive, inherited culture. According to cultural historian Georgina Boyes, "By the beginning of the 1930s, Folk culture had been fully colonised by the Revival. The Folk, on the verge of extinction at the turn of the century, could now be assumed to be nonexistent.... Revivalists had replaced the Folk, and constructed the population of rural areas as non-Folk—failed inheritors of the Folk's culture and artistic abilities." It was up to the academics to carry on these traditions, which they struggled to accomplish. "Although the status of the Folk as the well-spring of Englishness and national culture never came under concerted assault," she continues, "across a range of social, political and cultural positions there was a selective reduction in support for the institution and practices of the

Revival." By decade's end public interest in the dances of the EFDSS had substantially declined, and the organization languished.

The widespread economic collapse during the 1930s triggered radical political, social, as well as cultural movements, and thereby a search for authentic rural as well as urban working-class music, in order to draw from and connect with the people. Radical cultural organizations soon appeared, including the Workers' Theatre Movement. Workers' songs were nothing new, but now gained enhanced value, particularly as popularized by young cultural workers with a flair for organization and promotion. Composer Alan Bush led the formation of The Workers Music Association in 1936, dedicated to "the promotion of socialist and communist song from national and international sources." The group's prime goal was to elevate the working-class through promoting classical music, with scant interest in folk music (until after World War II); it had the support of modernist composers Benjamin Britten, Hans Eisler, and John Ireland.

Folk music from the United States, however, came to Britain through the mid-decade BBC radio broadcasts of Alistair Cooke. He traveled to the United States in 1932, and when briefly back in England in 1936 he produced a half-hour program for BBC on American hobo songs entitled "New York City to the Golden Gate." He emigrated permanently to the United States the following year and soon began a series of 13 programs for BBC entitled *I Heard American Singing*, which drew upon John and Alan Lomax's Library of Congress field recordings of work songs, from lumberjacks and railroad construction workers, and prison songs by African Americans. The program generated a positive response in the British press. Cooke soon met jazz legend Jelly Roll Morton in Washington, D.C. and was present for his lengthy, seminal-recording sessions with Alan Lomax at the Library of Congress. In the summer of 1939, western music star Gene Autry, most famous for his movie roles, was touring in Great Britain, performing in London, Liverpool, Glasgow, and Dublin. He received a warm welcome, with a cheering crowd of 300,000 lining the streets of Dublin as he rode by on his horse "Champion".

The outbreak of World War II prompted the start of a radio show, "Country Magazine," in May 1942 (until 1954), designed to promote a unified nationalism through presenting a broad folk culture through personal stories and traditional folk songs. Heard every other Sunday, the program's musical arranger, Francis Collinson, "recorded pub singers at the 'Eel's Foot' in Suffolk, hurdle makers in Dorset and Harry Cox in his woodshed." Scottish folk songs were well represented. Collecting Irish folk songs had grown out of the founding of the Irish Folklore Institute in 1930, changed to the Irish Folklore Commission in 1935, which sent story and song collectors throughout the countryside. Fieldworkers were helped by the publication of the *Handbook of Irish Folklore* in 1942.

FOLK MUSIC IN THE UNITED STATES DURING THE DEPRESSION

The depression in the United States, and the subsequent rise of the New Deal under President Franklin Roosevelt, created a healthy atmosphere for the growth and development of an interest in folk songs, and folk culture more broadly. All sorts of music flourished, from hard-bitten industrial songs to cowboy laments, from traditional ballads to new string-band compositions, blues with a political thrust, and just about anything else having to do with the "folk." That is, a folk consciousness took hold, as the country survived the hard times, with great difficulty, while emphasizing its traditional democratic values and hearty spirit. In 1927 104 million records were sold, but only 6 million in 1932. The smaller record companies collapsed, and the larger ones barely survived, but folk music could easily be heard over

ARCHIVE OF FOLK CULTURE

In 1928 Herbert Putnam, the Librarian of Congress, appointed Robert W. Gordon "specialist and consultant in the field of Folk Song and Literature" at the Library of Congress in Washington, D.C. A graduate of Harvard College, Gordon had been collecting and publishing folk songs for some years and seemed the perfect person to launch such an enterprise. As Carl Engel, chief of the library's Music Division, wrote at the time: "There is a pressing need for the formation of a great centralized collection of American folk-songs. ... This collection should comprise all the poems and melodies that have sprung from our soil or have been transplanted here, and have been handed down, often with manifold changes, from generation to generation as a precious possession of our folk." Engel's dream was more than fulfilled, as the Archive of American Folk-Song, as it was originally named, would grow throughout the century and into the next. Originally funded from private sources, it would not obtain public support for a few years.

Robert Gordon spent most of his time in the field, using a cumbersome recording machine, and was not an efficient administrator. John Lomax replaced Gordon in 1932 as "honorary curator." He also spent much of his time collecting field recordings, along with his son Alan, who became the archive's first federally funded full-time staff member in 1937, serving as "assistant in charge." John Lomax donated his recordings to the archive's growing collection in exchange for using their equipment. Alan remained as head of the archive until 1942. The growth of the archive was part of the New Deal's commitment, under the administration of President Franklin Roosevelt, to promoting cultural research and programs. Folklorist Ben Botkin served as head of the archive during the duration of World War II, 1942–1945, and was replaced by Duncan Emrich, also a Harvard trained folklorist, who served for ten years with the title "chief of the Folklore Section." The collection of field recordings had grown significantly, with contributions from collectors such as Vance Randolph, Eloise Hubbard Linscott, Zora Neale

Hurston, Herbert Halpert, Melville Hersokovits, and many others. A sample of these recordings began to appear on 78 rpm records issued by the Library's Recording Laboratory beginning in 1942, which were transferred to the 33 rpm LP format beginning in the early 1950s.

Emrich encouraged recording in other countries, and Arthur Alberts's work in West Africa, for example, helped to spread a greater understanding of African culture. Henrietta Yurchenco's field work in Mexico, Guatemala, Spain, Morocco, and Puerto Rico added a significant body of work to the library's expanding collection, with 10,000 discs by 1950, along with additional documentary materials. In 1955 Emrich's assistant, Rae Korson, was named head of the Folk Archive. The wife of folklorist George Korson, she remained until 1969, and was succeeded by Alan Jabbour, an academic who recorded southern fiddling traditions. With the swelling of the folk revival, the Folk Archive took on new importance with the growing interest in the country's folk heritage. After five years Jabbour moved to the Folk Arts Program of the National Endowment for the Arts and was replaced by Joe Hickerson, who had been Korson's assistant starting in 1963. Hickerson became active in collecting materials from the developing folk music revival, including publications, photos, and much else, and he promoted the release of fifteen albums in the rich Folk Music in America series.

In 1976 Congress established the American Folklife Center, as part of the Library of Congress, following energetic lobbying by folklorist Archie Green, which included the Archive of Folk Culture, named in 1981, which had been transferred from the Music Division to the center in 1978. Peggy Bulger replaced Jabbour as director of the American Folklife Center in 1999, and Michael Taft became head of the Folk Archive in 2002. The Folk Archive has become a central repository of a wide array of materials dealing with folk music and folk life, including obtaining the Alan Lomax collection in 2004. It has well fulfilled its original mission as the repository of the country's (and world's) cultural heritage.

the airwaves, in cowboy movies, at live concerts, on union picket lines, or picked up from sheet music, song folios, and the larger commercial songbooks. The government promoted the collection of field recordings from throughout the country. It was indeed a dynamic decade for collecting and disseminating the nation's rich cultural legacy.

John Lomax had abandoned his folk music collecting and publishing through the 1920s, but in 1932 he again found himself giving lectures about cowboy songs and planning a new book. Indeed, assisted particularly by his son Alan, the elderly Lomax, now in his midsixties, had begun a grueling schedule that lasted through the decade. He was named "Honorary Consultant" to the Archive of American Folk-Song at the Library of Congress in 1932, and while he had no salary, he could use the archive's valuable recording equipment and the prestige of representing the federal government. Most of his time would now be devoted to collecting folk songs through the South. He particularly liked prison camps, thinking that black prisoners, in particular, cut off from modern society and hardly tainted by popular music, served as a unique repository of traditional songs. This was a romantic and exaggerated view, but nonetheless served Lomax well in his search for interesting singers and songs. For example, he first met the gifted songster Huddie Ledbetter, better known as Lead Belly, at Angola Prison Farm in Louisiana in 1933.

Despite his busy schedule, and with the assistance of Alan, John Lomax managed to publish *American Ballads and Folk Songs* in 1934 (a second volume, *Our Singing Country*, followed in 1941). This was a rich collection of songs that focused on work and survival. "A life of isolation, without books or newspapers or telephone or radio, breeds songs and ballads," Lomax argued. "The gamut of human experiences has been portrayed through this unrecorded (at least until recently) literature of the people." Upon Lead Belly's release from prison in 1934, Lomax hired him as a driver and introduced him to northern audiences, where he performed the amazing repertoire of songs that would inspire generations of music fans. In 1936 John and Alan published *Negro Folk Songs As Sung by Lead Belly*. As John Lomax explained, "Alan and I were looking particularly for the songs of the Negro laborer, the words of which sometimes reflect the tragedies of imprisonment, cold, hunger, heat, the injustice of the white man. Fortunately for us and, it turned out, fortunately for him, Lead Belly had been fond of this type of songs."

The Lomaxes were not alone in publishing and promoting a wide variety of folk songs and ballads during these economically lean years, as the "folk" took on a new importance. Folklorists were energized to capture and highlight the country's democratic energy and vibrant cultures, and thankful for the government's offer of a job. "In this decade, Americans enthusiastically collected, presented, marketed, and consumed the nation's folkways, past and present," folklorist Jane Becker has argued. "The public encountered folk culture on festival and theater stages, over the radio and in recordings, at country fairs and museum exhibits, in popular magazines and published fiction, and through department stores and mail-order catalogs." This was particularly true regarding the South, where "writers, ballad hunters, and social workers in the mountains fostered the myth that a traditional American culture existed in Southern Appalachia," and where the Lomaxes, among many others, early focused their attention. The federal government, particularly through the Federal Writers' Project (FWP) and similar programs in the mid-1930s, sponsored cultural explorations and rejuvenation that looked back to a traditional, romanticized past as well as forward to a vibrant, multicultural, perhaps even socialist future. John Lomax, a political conservative, for a time served as the "National Advisor of Folklore and Folkways" for the Writers' Project, while his son, Alan, enthusiastically promoted a radical

ALAN LOMAX

Although performers and songwriters are the most familiar in any understanding of the history of folk music, it is also vital to have some awareness of those behind the scenes—the managers, record company owners, festival organizers, song collectors and publishers, etc.—who made the music accessible to the broader public. One of the most important, in both the United States and the British Isles, was Alan Lomax. Born on January 31, 1915, in Texas, for seven decades he contributed to the collection, academic study, understanding, and promotion of folk music. As a teenager he accompanied his father, John A. Lomax, on his southern collecting trips. He published his first article in 1934, and within a few years, in collaboration with his father, he published four influential folksong books, including *American Ballads and Folk Songs*, *Negro Folk Songs As Sung by Lead Belly*, and *Our Singing Country*. In 1937, the young Lomax was appointed director of the Archive of American Folk-Song at the Library of Congress, a position he held into the early 1940s. He led numerous field trips throughout the country, focusing on the South. Simultaneously, he had two CBS national radio shows, featuring Lead Belly, Woody Guthrie, the Golden Gate Quartet, Pete Seeger, and other developing folk performers.

Moving back and forth between Washington, D.C. and New York City, Lomax kept busy into the early 1940s with numerous recording, publishing, and radio projects. He had a particular knack for recording and promoting influential performers, including Lead Belly, Burl Ives, Josh White, Muddy Waters, Son House, and the jazz pioneer Jelly Roll Morton; his interviews with Morton later appeared in a ground-breaking oral history book, *Mister Jelly Roll* (1950). Lomax's commitment to left-wing politics was early apparent, as he assisted the activist Almanac Singers. He continued to work for the government during World War II, now in the Army producing shows for the Armed Forces Radio Service. At the war's end in 1945 he returned to producing folk records for Decca Records, wrote articles for popular magazines, such as *Vogue* and *The New York Times Magazine*, conducted a radio show on the Mutual network, and produced numerous concerts, all designed to promote folk music to a wide audience. He also connected with People's Songs, a national organization designed to link folk music with progressive politics, including promoting labor unions, international peace, and civil rights.

In 1950, motivated by his desire to avoid the escalating political repression in the United States and also to expand his collecting across the Atlantic, Lomax moved to England. He soon began field recording in Ireland, Scotland, and England, then moved on to Spain and Italy. He compiled a wealth of recordings from traditional singers, which became part of the influential seventeen volume Columbia (Records) World Library of Folk and Primitive Music. Simultaneously, he worked closely with numerous British collectors and performers, including A. L. Lloyd, Ewan MacColl, Hamish Henderson, Peter Kennedy, and Seamus Ennis. He continued with his radio work, now for the BBC's Third Programme, introducing the audience to American folk music as well as his European field recordings. While not know as a performer, Lomax was part of a skiffle group, the Ramblers, along with Peggy Seeger, MacColl, and Shirley Collins, and he recorded a few albums in both England and the United States. Indeed, Lomax played a vital role in stimulating a folk revival in England before his return to the United States in 1958. Back in New York City he plunged into the developing folk scene. He published the vital collection *The Folk Songs of North America* (1960) and served on the board of the Newport Folk Festival, although not without controversy due to his dominant personality and musical feelings. He also strongly supported the civil rights movement.

By the late 1960s, Lomax had become increasingly involved in formulating a complex and controversial interpretation of the world's folk music (called Cantrometrics) and dance (called Choreometrics), and he published extensively on these topics. His goal was a multimedia, cross-cultural computer database, which he named the Global Jukebox Project, uncompleted at his death on July 19, 2002. Following his death, as during much of his life, Lomax was recognized as a major influence on the development of folk music in the United States, the British Isles, even worldwide. Rounder Records has projected 150 CDs

> in its comprehensive Alan Lomax Collection. Through his numerous books and articles (anthologized as *Alan Lomax: Selected Writings, 1934–1997*, Cohen 2003), radio shows in the United States and England, collecting trips, concerts, recordings, and so much else, Alan Lomax remained a vital influence on developing and shaping a broad audience for folk and popular music for more than six decades.

agenda, in which preserving and promoting vernacular cultures represented a challenge to the power of capitalism.

Music scholar and ethnomusicologist Charles Seeger, also with left-wing politics, worked closely with John and Alan Lomax, Ben Botkin, and others through the federal government's various cultural programs. Seeger headed the Federal Music Project (FMP) of the Works Project Administration (WPA) from 1937 to 1941. He promoted increased recording of traditional singers for the Archive of American Folk-Song, and publication of the valuable *Check-List of Recorded Music in the English Language in the Archive of American Folksong*. In 1938 he joined with Ben Botkin, folklore editor for the FWP (succeeding John Lomax), in forming a Joint Committee on Folk Arts in order to better promote folk music collecting and scholarship, although it was short-lived because of cutbacks in federal programs. The Seeger and Lomax families were particularly close, with Ruth Crawford Seeger doing the musical transcriptions for the Lomaxes' *Our Singing Country*. Pete Seeger, the son of Charles and his first wife Constance, a budding banjo player and a Harvard College dropout, briefly worked for Alan Lomax at the Library of Congress in 1939, organizing the collections while learning numerous traditional folksongs, an invaluable education that he would soon put to good use.

COUNTRY MUSIC

Despite general economic hardships, historian Bill Malone has noted that "the most remarkable fact of country music's history during the Great Depression is that the music not only survived but expanded." While the record industry was limping along, traditional country musicians found work on the proliferating radio shows, particularly in the South, Midwest, and on the West Coast. "The typical hillbilly musician of that decade was an itinerant entertainer, moving from station to station, seeking sponsors and working a territory until it provided no further dividends." Some became major stars, such as Gene Autry, but most sustained a modest career, if not more, on radio programs such as the National Barn Dance (WLS in Chicago), the Grand Ole Opry (WSM in Nashville), the Old-Fashioned Barn Dance (KMOX, Saint Louis), the Crazy Barn Dance (WBT, Charlotte), the Renfro Valley Barn Dance (WHAS in Louisville), and the Boone County Jamboree (WLW in Cincinnati). The Coon Creek Girls, Bradley Kincaid, Karl Davis and Harty Taylor, Bill and Charlie Monroe, the Blue Sky Boys, Roy Acuff, and dozens of others became established performers. The very popular Carter Family also appeared on a few powerful stations located just across the border in Mexico. While most of the hillbilly radio shows were located in the South, they could often be heard throughout the country. Economic hardships, compounded by fierce dust storms, uprooted many from the Midwest, who relocated to California and established a thriving country music market. Singing movie cowboys proliferated, led by Gene Autry, Tex Ritter, and the Sons of the Pioneers, as the film industry catered to country/western music fans throughout the country.

Professional musicians competed for audience attention on records, radio programs, and concert stages, but many others, with less commercial potential, nonetheless managed to appear at the numerous folk festivals and amateur shows. "On a local scale, in thousands of schoolhouses throughout the Southeast, rural white southerners continued to gather and listen to the performances of musicians often raised in nearby communities," historian Jeffrey Lange has written. Festivals were another outlet for budding performers. Bascom Lamar Lunsford, a flamboyant lawyer, traditional musician, and folk song collector, initiated the Mountain Dance and Folk Festival in Asheville, North Carolina, in 1930, which he directed until the 1970s. Attracting dancers and musicians from Western North Carolina, the festival initially featured unaccompanied ballad singers, as well as banjo players and fiddlers. Fiddle and banjo contests and conventions had been held in North Carolina since 1905, often in schoolhouses; the Union Grove Fiddlers' Convention began in 1924. Such indoor conventions somewhat declined following World War II.

Folk festivals soon spread. Jean Thomas, a rather prolific collector and author of folk song books, started the American Folk Song Festival in her hometown of Ashland, Kentucky, in 1931. She had a very traditional approach to the idea. "The children in the valleys, in the foothills, and in the mountains should be given the opportunity of hearing the ballads of their forebears," she would write in her fanciful autobiography, *The Sun Shines Bright* (1940). She believed "only those mountain minstrels to whom the ballads had been handed down by word of mouth should participate. Only those untrained fiddlers and musicians who had learned their art from their forebears should take part." Annabel Morris Buchanan had a similar idea when she initiated the White Top Folk Festival in Southwest Virginia, also in 1931. A "folk festival should encourage only the highest type of native material, traditionally learned and traditionally presented," she explained in 1937, just two years before her festival ended. She did not exclude more recent compositions, if "the structure or literary merit of the text may entitle it to consideration beyond that of the folklorist alone, ... or perhaps the tune is derived from some older folk air." That is, the festival was "held for the purpose of discovering, preserving, and carrying on the best native [white] music, balladry, dances, traditions, and other arts and customs that belong to our race." Eleanor Roosevelt, wife of the president, visited in 1933. The next year the festival attracted 200 performers and 10,000 fans, and featured a conference with professional folklorists discussing the current state of folk song collecting. Douglas Kennedy and Maud Karpeles, directors of the English Folk Song and Dance Society, sent their congratulations, and in 1935 sword and morris dances were added to the program. The last festival was held in 1939. Folklorist Jane Becker has criticized many of the festival promoters for their narrow views: "They proceeded to sanitize culture, weeding out the vulgar and the crude and presenting only those forms that upheld their middle-class standards of propriety and taste. Annabel Morris Buchanan argued that festivals should encourage only the 'highest type of native material.' Modern chain-gang songs, hillbilly tunes, and humorous songs, she rejected, not because of their contemporary nature, but because of their crudeness and vulgarity."

Sarah Gertrude Knott, from Kentucky, attended Bascom Lamar Lunsford's 1934 festival, and was inspired to immediately start the National Folk Festival in St. Louis. But her concept of folk culture was somewhat different from the white-centered, rural nostalgia of Jean Thomas, Annabel Morris Buchanan, and Lunsford. Groups from 14 states participated in the first National Folk Festival, representing "the traditional heritages rooted here in early days and those that have grown up I [sic] our country," she later explained. But this meant including "the Indians, British, Spanish-Americans, French, German, and Negroes, along with the newer indigenous creations of the cowboy, lumberjack, sailor, and other such typical groups." The second festival, held in Chattanooga, Tennessee, in 1935, featured mountain fiddlers and ballad singers, as well as Pennsylvania

anthracite miners, and a thousand-voice black chorus singing spirituals. The yearly National Folk Festival would continue its unique, eclectic approach to the country's complex
folk traditions throughout the century.

Throughout the decade folk music and dance from around
the world was commonly performed and celebrated. The Folk
Festival Council of New York City, for example, was formed
in 1932, "not only to give the people of our land opportunities to enjoy the contributions of our foreign born groups to
the folk arts, but to keep those arts alive as a vital part of our
community life." The council published *Folk-News*, which
covered local events as well as the National Folk Festivals
and folk life exhibits at the New York World's Fair in 1939.
Moreover, ethnic choruses and dancers appeared at music
festivals and pageants sponsored by various organizations,
including the Communist Party, which comprised various
nationality organizations and an international outlook. For
example, the Festival of the American Music League in 1936
included the German Workers Club Chorus and the Ukrainian Workers Chorus, along with composer Aaron Copland
playing his own compositions.

George Korson, newspaperman and collector of miners' songs, organized the short-lived Pennsylvania Folk
Festival in 1935, which represented the varied nature of
the state's people. The 1936 festival included Chief Strong
Fox and his Seneca Indians doing tribal dances, Ukrainian
folk dances, gypsy music, French and German folk songs,
African-American spirituals, miners' songs and ballads, sea
chanteys, and even Stephen Foster songs. In 1936 Korson
organized five regional festivals, leading up to the major festival held at Bucknell University's Memorial Stadium. This
was a mammoth affair, again featuring the state's various
cultures, even including Gypsy folk music and the lore of
the vanished lumber and river rafting industries. Korson's
wide-ranging, imaginative festival ended in 1938, having
run into financial and other difficulties, but it indicated the

possibilities of including the country's mix of musical and folk cultures.

While commercial radio programs and Hollywood movies, along with stage shows, the crippled record industry, even folk festivals, created economic possibilities for white performers, African Americans had few such outlets or opportunities. There was one attempt at the all-black Fort Valley State College near Macon, Georgia. Folk music was originally included in a festival designed to teach young people an appreciation of music in 1940, with W. C. Handy as the judge. The next year a separate folk festival was organized, which would soon include guitar, banjo, and harmonica players, string bands, along with singers, doing both secular (blues) and sacred songs. The Library of Congress recorded some of the early festivals, which finally ended in the mid-1950s.

Blues performers continued to do some recording, although greatly limited, and performing through the Depression years. Radio and records had become widespread throughout the South by the 1930s, for both whites and blacks, with all sorts of music available, but the recording companies were only interested in what they considered music that was seemingly unique to the African-American population. As Elijah Wald has notably argued, "radio exposed blues players, and rural listeners in general, to other styles. It was a great leveler, allowing someone in a Delta cabin to listen to anything from hillbilly fiddling to opera." Muddy Waters (aka McKinley Morganfield), first recorded by Alan Lomax and John Work in 1941 on the Stovall plantation, for example, "listed more [Gene] Autry hits in his repertoire than songs by any blues artist." Wald has been pretty much alone among blues historians in attempting to position the blues within the larger context of popular music. In *Escaping the Delta* he has made a strong argument that "rural black Delta dwellers were not only aware of all sorts of nonblues, non-Mississippi music, but were doing their best to keep up with the latest developments." Robert Johnson has become the most famous of the Delta musicians, but it must be noted that he only recorded 29 songs in 1936 and 1937, and died in 1938 not long after his records were barely available. His fame remained local until the 1960s.

If the blues was only one musical style popular in the Mississippi Delta, it was also the case throughout the rest of the South, where there was much greater urban growth and industrial expansion. There was a vibrant blues marketplace in the Southeast beginning in the 1920s, for example, well documented by Bruce Bastin in *Red River Blues*, with the likes of Blind Willie McTell, Buddy Moss, Blind Boy Fuller, and Blind Gary Davis, as well as Brownie McGhee and Sonny Terry. Texas also had its share of blues musicians, including Blind Lemon Jefferson, who died in 1930, Texas Alexander, and the versatile Huddie Ledbetter (aka Lead Belly). In Memphis bandleader W. C. Handy, the self-proclaimed "father of the blues," held forth, along with the Beale Street Sheiks, Memphis Minnie and Joe McCoy, the Memphis Jug Band, and Gus Cannon's Jug Stompers. The blues could take many forms—solo guitar and piano players, jug bands, duos, blues shouters, the classic blues singers such as Bessie Smith. Many performers, such as Mississippi-born Big Bill Broonzy, were brought North to record in Chicago, Richmond, Indiana, or New York by the 1930s.

Blues was usually considered to reflect personal struggles and experiences, with little (or perhaps very subtle) larger political implications. There was, however, a large body of blues and gospel songs of an overt political nature, although the Lomaxes and most other collectors seemed not to notice. For example, President Franklin Roosevelt had won the support of most African Americans by 1934, although those who lived in the South were unable to vote, which generated a large body of songs, but not all were uncritical. Van Rijn (1997) has carefully documented the story in *Roosevelt's Blues: African-American Blues and Gospel Songs On FDR*. Big Bill Broonzy, for example, praised the WPA in his "WPA Rag," as did Casey Bill Weldon in "W.P.A. Blues," while Peetie Wheatstraw countered with "304 Blues (Lost My Job on the Project)." In 1938 Lead Belly recorded the critical "Bourgeois Blues" about segregation in Washington, D.C., although he also wrote "The Roosevelt Song" which was positive about the president. Lawrence Gellert, who had moved to North Carolina from New York in 1924, had earlier managed to collect a number of political, even militant, blues, which were first published in the Communist sponsored *New Masses* magazine, and collected in *Negro Songs of Protest* (1936). "These songs are still in the making," he noted in the Preface. "Never sung twice quite in the same way, new verses are constantly improvised, the text doggerel, nonsense, bawdy or protest, depending upon the mood of the singers or whether whites are within earshot."

Just as black performers were exposed to a wide range of white musical styles, the opposite was also true, that white musicians were often influenced by the blues. The Allen Brothers, for example, recorded "Chattanooga Blues" in 1927, but when it was listed in the Columbia Records race catalog they threatened to sue the company for damaging their reputations (listeners would think they were black). They were not alone in adopting a blues style, including Frank Hutchinson, Tom Darby and Jimmie Tarlton, and particularly Jimmie Rodgers, whose "blue yodels" were highly influential, particularly on the young Gene Autry. "As the 1930s drew to a close, the blues was assimilated into more and more forms of commercial country music," Charles Wolfe has written. "The notion of white blues was no longer novel, and producers no longer thought of it as an automatic ticket to big sales, but it was on its way to becoming a part of the deep fabric of country music."

FOLK MUSIC SCHOLARSHIP AND POPULARITY

The diverse scholarly songbooks that continued to appear through the Depression captured some of the decade's cultural/musical dynamic. While much of the attention continued to focus on the South, folklorists were scattered throughout the country, finding older ballads and folk songs wherever they searched. For example, Margaret Larkin published *Singing Cowboy* in 1931. While she cautioned the reader that "Cowboy songs are not folk songs in the scholarly sense of the word. Nearly all of them are parodies of old ballads or of popular songs of their day," but they should now be considered part of the folk heritage. She does note, however, "Radio singers and phonograph recordings have popularized cowboy songs, of late years, and have not been without their effect on the folk singers.... The authority of the record sometimes shakes the folk singers' confidence in their local versions, but revives their interest in the old songs, and their belief in their worth and dignity."

This would be a common problem for all collectors, trying to separate modern influences from traditional words and performance styles. While New England folk songs and ballads have not been particularly well known, compared to those from the South, numerous collections were published, including Helen with George Brown, *Vermont Folk-Songs and Ballads* (1931); Phillips Barry, *The Maine Woods Songster* (1939); Eloise Hubbard Linscott, *Folk Songs of Old New England* (1939). Traditional songs were fading from vernacular culture, but could still be discovered by zealous collectors. As Jennifer Post has recently noted, in *Music in Rural New England Family and Community Life, 1870–1940*: "By the 1930s and 1940s, musical standards for many people in this region [Northern New England] were set by national radio programs and the hillbilly song industry.... For many people these newer traditions became a source for family tradition, supplanting older practices."

The New England collectors were joined by George Pullen Jackson, who produced *Spiritual Folk-Songs of Early America* (1937). George Korson documented coal mining songs in *Minstrels of the Mine Patch* (1938). The Midwest was now covered, for example, by Mary Eddy's *Ballads and Songs From Ohio* (1939), and the numerous southern collections included Harvey Fuson's *Ballads of the Kentucky Highlands* (1931). The government, through the Federal Theatre Project, issued Robert Gordon's *Folk-Songs of America* in 1938, drawn from his earlier *New York Times* articles.

There were also scores of country and western songs appearing in sheet music and song portfolios, many of recent vintage, and featuring both popular and obscure musicians. The major performers, such as the Carter Family, Jimmie Rodgers, and Gene Autry, had numerous printed collections, but seemingly so did every other performer. The M. M. Cole Publishing Company offered a wide range of songbooks, including *Carson J. Robison's World's Greatest Collection of Mountain Ballads and Old Time Songs* (1930), *Elmore Vincent's Lumber Jack Songs* (1932), as well as compilations by the Ranch Boys, Doc Hopkins and Karl and Harty, Happy Jack Turner, and many others. American Music, Inc. also published a broad list of performers, such as the Drifting Pioneers, Al Clauser and His Oklahoma Outlaws, "Dude" Martin, Bill Boyd, and the Tennessee Ramblers. The sale of song folios was profitable not only for the publishers but also the performers, serving as their publicity. Most of their songs were newly written or arranged, thus supplying royalties for the composers or arrangers, as well as the publishers. Moreover, the proliferation of song folios indicated that the audience for folk music was not content just to listen to the radio or attend a concert, but was also singing the songs at home and/or with friends.

ALAN LOMAX AND PEOPLE'S MUSIC

Alan Lomax combined the zeal of the collector, the commitments of a social and political activist, keen musical sensibilities, and the backing of the federal government. Born in 1915, and a graduate of the University of Texas, Alan had assisted his father in 1933, the same year he published his first article, "Collecting Folk-Songs of the Southern Negro." After collecting songs in the Georgia Sea Islands and Haiti, in 1937 he was appointed director of the Archive of American Folk-Song at the Library of Congress and immediately began his collecting travels through Kentucky, Indiana, Ohio, Michigan, and Vermont. He recorded hundreds of songs for the Library of Congress.

He also launched a radio series for CBS's *American School of the Air* in late 1939, aimed at children, which was quickly followed by the adult-oriented *Back Where I Come From*. Lomax introduced the public to Lead Belly, Woody Guthrie, Josh White, Burl Ives, the Golden Gate Quartet, and Pete Seeger. Always on the go, with seemingly unlimited energy and a creative spirit, he recorded lengthy interviews with Woody Guthrie, Lead Belly, jazz pioneer Jelly Roll Morton, and Aunt Molly Jackson, the wife of a Kentucky coal miner who wrote vivid songs about their terrible living conditions, for the Library of Congress. He was anxious to document not only the most traditional black and white performers, but also those using folk styles to explore contemporary topics, such as Guthrie, who captured the plight of the rural poor displaced from their farms in Oklahoma who moved to California. Born in 1912, Woody would become, with Lomax's help, a significant composer and musical influence. His "This Land Is Your Land" eventually became the unofficial national anthem, but not until the 1960s, just before his death in 1967.

Lomax traveled throughout the country recording traditional songs and ballads from scores of singers, which he dutifully deposited in the Library of Congress. But he was also promoting and encouraging newly written topical songs that would advocate labor unions, civil rights, world peace, and generally challenge the status quo. He was part and parcel of the upsurge during the Depression of grass-roots organizing as well as an increased interest, at all levels, in the country's folk culture. Michael Denning (1996) has tried to capture this broad tendency in *The Cultural Front*: "The result of the encounter between a powerful democratic social movement—the Popular Front—and the modern cultural apparatuses of mass entertainment and education." He continues: "For the first time in the history of the United States, a working-class culture had made a significant imprint on the dominant cultural institutions…. Vernacular musics like jazz, blues, and country resonated around the world." That is, folk music had moved from the undercurrents of society into the mainstream, where it would continue, off and on, throughout the century.

Labor/activist songs had existed throughout the nineteenth century, from worker and abolitionist tunes to farmers' laments and spirituals, and more overtly political songs connected with union and agrarian upheavals. They appeared in scores of songsters and broadsides, while others turned up in labor publications. By the early twentieth century there was a strong legacy of using songs for labor organizing purposes, although the connection to the folk was sometimes tenuous. The Industrial Workers of the World (IWW or Wobblies), a radical labor movement, used popular song melodies, as well as familiar religious tunes, to carry their musical messages. The IWW first published *Songs of the Workers: On the Road in the Jungles and in the Shops* in 1909. Better known as "The Little Red Song Book", it was small enough to fit into a shirt or back pocket and traveled the length of the land, spreading the songs of Joe Hill ("Casey Jones—The Union Scab"), T-Bone Slim ("I'm Too Old to Be a Scab"), Ralph Chaplin ("Paint 'Er Red," to the tune of "Marching Through Georgia"), as well as "The Marseillaise" and "The Internationale." ("The Little Red Song Book" is still in print.) The Socialist Party also printed songbooks, as did various labor unions by the 1930s, filled with a variety of labor-oriented tunes, old and new.

The formation of the Congress of Industrial Organizing (CIO) after 1935 reflected and sparked the rise of union activism among industrial workers in steel, auto, rubber, mining, and numerous other workplaces. While union organizers were not particularly interested in using folk tunes in their organizing drives, an emerging number of Communist Party-USA (CP-USA) members and activists, within and beyond the emerging labor unions, found traditional musical styles useful. The CP-USA had formed in 1919, but had been a fringe group until the mid-1930s, when it joined with other left/labor groups in a Popular Front to promote antifascism, civil rights, and union organizing. Both the CP-USA and individual CIO unions published numerous songbooks (although officially the Communist Party had little interest in folk music). The songs were designed to create a union consciousness as well as solidarity during strikes and on picket lines. The *Red Song Book* (1932) included IWW tunes such as "The Preacher and the Slave," "Hold the Fort," and Aunt Molly Jackson's "Poor Miner's Farewell." By decade's end there were numerous labor/left songs and songbooks that captured a militant movement and spirit. Simultaneously, the Spanish Civil War (1936–1939) generated many folk-style songs supporting the Republican government and opposing the army/Catholic church rebellion that had the backing of Nazi Germany and Fascist Italy.

Labor unions and labor schools continued publishing songbooks through the decade. For example, the *Brookwood Chautauqua Songs* booklet, from the later 1930s, published in Katonah, New York, with the slogan "A Singing Army Is a Winning Army," began with "Solidarity Forever," and included "Victory Song of the Dressmakers," "The Soup Song," and "March Song of the Workers." *Commonwealth Labor Songs*, appearing in 1938, included a similar lineup, beginning with "The Internationale," and ending with "Old John Lewis" (to the tune of "Old MacDonald Had a Farm"). Folk-styled songs had become the norm by the middle of the Depression, catchy lyrics with familiar traditional or popular tunes and hymns that would be easily remembered and sung. *CIO Songs*, issued by the Birmingham Industrial Union Council, began with "the C.I.O's in Dixie" (to the tune of "Dixie"), and continued with "The Workers' Marseillaise," "The Steel Workers' Battle Hymn" (to the tune of "Hold the Fort"), and "We Have Fed You All for a Thousand Years." *Songs For America: American Ballads, Folk Songs, Marching Songs, Songs of Other Lands* appeared in 1939, a rich, varied collection that seemed to sum up the range of songs that appealed to a singing Left, beginning appropriately with "The Star Spangled Banner," immediately followed by "The Internationale," some Spanish Civil War tunes, "Kevin Barry," and "The Ballad of the Chicago Steel Massacre." The same year Zilphia Horton compiled *Labor Songs* for the Textile Workers Union. Various unions continued to issue small songbooks into the next decade. During the war the Educational Department of the International Ladies Garment Workers Union (ILGWU) published *Everybody Sings* (1942), about the same time the New York State Federation of Teachers Unions issued *Sing with the Union*, along with the UAW-CIO Education Department's *UAW-CIO Sings*.

Rural protest songs, white and black, reached northern audiences through the labors of various Left-oriented collectors, publicists, and performers. The Memphis-born, New York-based songwriter, publisher, and performer Bob Miller waxed scores of such songs, although he was better known in radical circles for his compositions, such as "11 Cent Cotton, Forty Cent Meat," and for his publication of the portfolio *Songs of the Almanac Singers* (1942). Margaret Larkin, a poet and journalist, born in New Mexico and raised with cowboy songs, also linked folk songs and social protest. She publicized the songs and struggles of Ella May Wiggins, who had been gunned down in 1929 during the Gastonia textile strike, and early befriended Aunt Molly Jackson. Larkin performed Ella May's "The Mill Mother's Lament" and other labor songs in New York during the early 1930s. Composers and performers Florence Reese, Ella May Wiggins, Jim Garland, his half-sister Aunt Molly Jackson and sister Sarah Ogan Gunning, Woody Guthrie, Agnes "Sis" Cunningham, Lee Hays, and John Handcox soon captured a mix of native radical politics and working-class trials and hardships. They often identified with such Left-led unions as the National Miners Union, the National Textile Workers, and the Southern Tenant Farmers Union (STFU). There were also labor-oriented

WOODY GUTHRIE

"This Land Is Your Land" has become the unofficial national anthem of the United States since the 1950s, often learned by students in public school and heard frequently at public functions. But while the song is very familiar, its composer, Woody Guthrie, is hardly known, although he became a member of the Rock and Roll Hall of Fame in 1988, and appeared on a U.S. postage stamp in 1998. By the 1960s he had become the prototype of the creative singer/songwriter, combining folk music and protest lyrics. He also penned catchy children's songs, and his erratic lifestyle captivated a generation of restless young people, such as Bob Dylan. Woodrow Wilson Guthrie was born on July 14, 1912, in Okemah, Oklahoma, the son of Charles and Nora Belle Guthrie. Charley Guthrie sold real estate and held local office, and the family was generally well off until the early 1920s. But hard times came, and then Nora Guthrie was permanently hospitalized because of Huntington's chorea, a hereditary disease that would eventually incapacitate Woody. By his late teens Woody, a voracious reader and a budding artist and musician, was on his own. He married Mary Jennings in 1933 and their family quickly grew.

Always on the move, Woody relocated to Los Angeles in 1937 and soon launched a radio show with Maxine Crissman, who was best known as Lefty Lou. He had already begun writing songs, such as "Talking Dust Bowl" and "Oklahoma Hills," usually borrowing his tunes from gospel or traditional songs, with the words based on his experiences or news stories. He began developing a local reputation as a folk performer and clever composer. As the Depression dragged on, Woody became politically radical, soon connecting with the local Communist Party. He moved to New York City in early 1940 and appeared in the gala fundraising "Grapes of Wrath Evening," joining numerous local folk music activists: Alan and Bess Lomax, Aunt Molly Jackson, Lead Belly, the Golden Gate Quartet, and Pete Seeger. Alan Lomax, head of the Archive of American Folk-Song at the Library of Congress, soon had Woody recording hours of songs and stories for the Archive. He also appeared on Lomax's two CBS radio shows, as well as Henrietta Yurchenco's local folk program on WNYC; he even briefly had his own network show. During the busy year of 1940 he recorded two albums for Victor Records entitled *Dust Bowl Ballads*. While he continued to travel around the country, he did take some time to join the Almanac Singers, with Pete Seeger, Millard Lampell, and Lee Hays, who performed and recorded topical and traditional folk songs. He divorced Mary and later married Marjorie Mazia; together they had four children. His inventive autobiography, *Bound for Glory*, was published by Dutton in 1943, to generally positive reviews. Woody had already written "This Land Is Your Land" in 1940, as a political counter to Irving Berlin's "God Bless America."

In 1943, Woody joined the merchant marine with his close friends Cisco Houston and Jimmy Longhi; they survived three voyages carrying troops and cargo to Europe. In early 1945 he began recording on the Asch label, initiating a relationship with owner Moses "Moe" Asch that would result in numerous influential albums on what later became Folkways Records. Oddly, considering his age and numerous children, Woody was drafted and inducted into the army on May 7, 1945, the day Germany surrendered. He remained in camp until discharged in late December. He moved with Marjorie to Coney Island, where they would live until his hospitalization in the early 1950s. He continued to write songs at a rapid pace, as well as recording for Moe Asch, but his public fame had faded. He performed for various political causes and labor unions, but these opportunities were drying up by the late 1940s and left-wing politics was becoming increasingly unpopular. Guthrie disappeared from the national spotlight even before his permanent hospitalization by 1956, as he continued to physically deteriorate from Huntington's disease. He died on October 3, 1967.

When Woody died, his life and songs had already become a vital part of the developing folk music revival. Bob Dylan was highly influenced by Woody's recordings and maverick lifestyle, and visited with him on his move to New York City in 1961. Within a few years Woody became the most important influence on the folk movement, as a songwriter and activist. The 1988 HBO video and companion CD, *Folkways: A Vision Shared*, paired Woody and Lead Belly in a tribute featuring U2, Little Richard, Bruce Springsteen, Bob Dylan, Brian Wilson, and Willie Nelson, demonstrating the reach of Woody's and Lead Belly's songs. Indeed, Springsteen and Dylan carried on Woody's musical and political legacy, along with his son Arlo Guthrie. The British rocker Billy Bragg along with the rock group Wilco issued two albums of Woody's previously unrecorded songs entitled *Mermaid Avenue*, which reached a broad audience. While his creative career was very short, spanning less than a decade, from the late 1930s to the late 1940s, Woody's musical legacy and influence has continued to expand since the 1960s through the ongoing release of recordings by Smithsonian Folkways Recordings and numerous public events.

schools, such as the Highlander Folk School in Monteagle, Tennessee, Commonwealth College in Mena, Arkansas, the Southern School for Workers near Ashland, North Carolina, and the socialist Brookwood Labor School in Katonah, New York, which encouraged singing and published labor songbooks. Handcox penned "Ragged, Ragged Are We" and "There Are Mean Things Happening in This Land" while an organizer for the Socialist-connected STFU.

By the early 1940s there were a variety of labor-oriented records available by Josh White, Tony Kraber, and Earl Robinson. The Almanac Singers, however, were the first consciously organized and recorded singing group concerned with stimulating a singing labor movement. Formed by Pete Seeger, Lee Hays, and Millard Lampell in early 1941, they first recorded an album of controversial peace songs, *Songs for John Doe*, early in the year, closely followed by *Talking Union*, full of catchy labor songs that would long resonate in folk circles. "Folklore might be entertaining, it described the roots and aspirations of the masses," Richard Reuss has explained, "yet for most radicals it bore little relation to the realities of daily living in the urban and progressive milieus." The Almanac Singers, however, "attempted to implement a proletarian culture based on American traditions." While they lasted only two years, they laid the foundations for a singing progressive movement that would grow in the future, particularly in the 1960s. Other catchall labor-oriented groups recorded during World War II, including the Priority Ramblers and the Union Boys (Burl Ives, Josh White, Pete Seeger, Tom Glazer, Brownie McGhee, and Sonny Terry). Woody Guthrie also recorded labor songs during the war, further developing a body of music that would express a labor consciousness and progressive orientation. Reuss has labeled these performers the "Lomax singers," because Alan Lomax promoted and shaped their musical styles and repertoires: "In sum, while individual attitudes and outlooks varied within the Lomax tradition, folk music was regarded as considerably more than entertainment with a 'progressive' flavor or as a new agit-prop strategy." Rather, "it was the true 'people's' music of the United States, the rightful heritage of American workers." Lomax was heavily responsible for shaping the careers of Woody Guthrie, Lead Belly, Burl Ives, Josh White, and Pete Seeger, among others, the most significant and influential performers appearing after the war.

A. L. (BERT) LLOYD

Albert Lancaster "Bert" Lloyd was born in London in 1908. He was early exposed to folk music, through the singing of his parents, although both were dead by the time he was 15. He soon moved to Australia, where he worked on a sheep and cattle ranch for the next decade, and also became exposed to the songs of the sheep-and-cattle hands, shearers, and itinerant swagmen who moved around doing odd jobs, which he avidly collected. Self-educated, he returned to England in 1934, where he met radical writers, joined the Communist Party, and struggled to survive during hard times. He cultivated a broad knowledge of English folk songs, joining a growing movement which included the founding of the Workers' Music Association. He finally found work on a whaling ship for a seven-month trip to the Antarctic, which was followed by work on a freighter; he picked up numerous shanties, whaling songs, and other sea songs. He also began to write scripts for the BBC, starting with "The Voice of the Seamen," which launched his career as a radio broadcaster and journalist.

He expanded his interest in folk songs, including cowboy songs from the United States, with an emphasis on the music of working people and the labor movement. He developed a Marxist view of the history of folk music, which appeared in his article "The Revolutionary Origins of English Folk-Song" in 1943, with an emphasis on the connection between music and economic classes. He expanded his ideas about the history of the topic the next year in the booklet *The Singing Englishman*. He soon began publishing songbooks, such as *Twelve Russian Folk Songs* (1945) and *Corn on the Cob* (1945), in which he praised the living tradition of folk music in the United States, including protest and workers' songs. In the 1950s he was working with Ewan MacColl in a variety of projects, including recordings, as he pursued his research that eventually resulted in *Folksong in England* (1967), the first and to date most comprehensive history of the subject. He had returned to radio production, including the series *Ballads and Blues* (1953), and later worked with MacColl on the

Radio Ballads. His editing (with composer Ralph Vaughn Williams) of *The Penguin Book of English Folk Songs* (1959) set a high standard that remains today. He recorded a series of albums with MacColl for Topic, and appeared on various other albums, including *A Selection from the Penguin Book of English Folk Songs, The Iron Muse, The Best of A.L. Lloyd, Haul on the Bowlin, Off to Sea Once More, The Unfortunate Rake*, and much more. He remained a vital force in the folk revival almost until his death in 1982, appearing at numerous folk festivals and conferences, where his unique voice and encyclopedic knowledge of folk songs were most influential. One summary of his life calls him "the most influential and revered figure in [the] post-war folk revival."

WORLD WAR II

In both Great Britain and the United States, World War II provided an upsurge in drawing upon folk music in underpinning the democratic challenge to militant fascism, as well as undercutting organized support for cultural programs. "The war had provided acceptability and a national platform for songs of anti-Fascist resistance—and initially left-wing groups such as the Workers' Music Association, Clarion Ramblers and various Co-Operative Society choirs were the only performers whose repertoires contained suitable material," Georgina Boyes has written about England. And she continues: "National songs in a range of languages, 'folk-songs, madrigals, freedom songs, variety numbers and some classical pieces,' as well as newly composed political songs were the standard fare at concerts and broadcasts devised by such organizations." The Workers' Music Association published a series of paperback books connecting music and culture, including A. L. Lloyd's *The Singing Englishman* (1944). Lloyd (1908–1982), with a labor background and membership in the Communist Party, highlighted songs from sailors and farmers, and argued that folk songs basically came from the lower classes, they were "something that came out of social upheaval."

FOLKWAYS RECORDS

Among the record companies that issued and promoted a wide range of folk recordings in the United States, Folkways Records was the most prolific. Moses "Moe" Asch (1905–1986), a recording engineer, began recording in 1939 on the Asch label, and from 1943 to 1945 joined with Herbert Harris to form the Asch/Stinson label, specializing in folk and jazz recordings. They released records by Woody Guthrie, Lead Belly, Josh White, Sonny Terry, Burl Ives, Coleman Hawkins, and Mary Lou Williams. Asch next launched the Disc label, which, following bankruptcy, became Folkways Records in 1948. Moe Asch had an expansive view of his new company, which would eventually issue more than 2,000 albums, including music and spoken word recordings from throughout the world, none of which would ever be deleted from the catalog.

Folkways' scope was indeed large. Some performers, such as Woody Guthrie, Lead Belly, Pete Seeger, and Ella Jenkins, appeared on numerous records, while others only once. An origins of jazz series was launched in 1950, quickly joined by a five-volume *Music of the World's People*, Seeger's extensive *American Ballads* series, and Harry Smith's influential three-volume *Anthology of American Folk Music* (1952). The *Anthology*'s collection of 84 scarce recordings of black and white rural southern music from the 1920s and 1930s influenced a new generation of folk music enthusiasts. Among the latter were John Cohen, Tom Paley, and Mike Seeger, who formed the New Lost City Ramblers and began recording for Asch in 1958, a relationship that would last for many years. The Ramblers kicked off a northern revival of southern roots and string-band music that would be fueled by Folkways release of numerous traditional performers, including Clarence "Tom" Ashley, Doc Watson, Jean Ritchie, Elizabeth "Libba" Cotten, and such compilation albums as *Mountain Music of Kentucky*, *Mountain Music Bluegrass Style*, and *The Country Blues*. Throughout the 1960s Folkways issued a steady stream of albums, such as *Drums of the Yoruba of Nigeria*, *2,000 Years of Music*, and numerous *Broadside* albums including a range of contemporary singer/songwriters, such as Bob Dylan, Eric Andersen, Peter LaFarge, Janis Ian, and Phil Ochs.

As the folk music revival reached its peak in the mid-1960s, Asch broadened his reach by briefly joining with Verve Records, a subsidiary of MGM, to reach a wider market. Some of the artists on the Verve/Folkways label were Lead Belly, Cisco Houston, Pete Seeger, Dock Boggs, and Lightnin' Hopkins. While Asch was not much of a political activist, he issued numerous radical/protest albums, including the reissue of the Almanac Singers' *Talking Union*, Pete Seeger's various topical albums, and a host of civil rights compilations by Guy Carawan, including *The Nashville Sit-In Story*, *We Shall Overcome: Songs of the "Freedom Riders" and the "Sit-Ins,"* and *The Story of Greenwood, Mississippi*.

Throughout the 1970s the Folkways output declined, as Asch struggled to continue the label, often with lesser names and sometimes odd titles, such as *The English Concertina, Irish Music from Cleveland, The World Music Theatre of Jon Appleton,* and Jeff Ampolsk's *God, Guns and Guts.* In 1984 an ailing Asch began negotiations to sell the company to the Smithsonian Institution, a transaction completed shortly after his death in 1986. Always existing on a financial shoestring, Moe Asch had managed to create a lasting monument to the world of recorded music and sound. He had issued some of the most influential folk performers and albums, all of which are still available from Smithsonian Folkways Recordings, which has also issued a steady stream of new compilations, such as *The Best of Broadside, 1962–1988: Anthems of the American Underground from the Pages of Broadside Magazine* (2000).

(The following year he explored vernacular music across the Atlantic in *Corn on the Cob: Popular and Traditional Poetry of the U.S.A.*: "The most of them—and this is the great characteristic of American folksongs—are the songs of men at work.") He would soon become a key influence in the British folk revival.

American music, including folk songs, came to Britain also through the broadcasts over BBC of U.S.-made records, and also programs from the Armed Forces Network (AFN), beginning in 1943. The following year the BBC, AFN, and

the Canadian Broadcasting Company formed the Allied
Expeditionary Forces Programme (AEFP), which aired
American swing bands and other pop music to a military
as well as civilian audience. Moreover, American troops
brought their own records, which further spread their music
throughout Britain. The BBC also aired a few traditional
singers, such as Harry Cox, to help promote patriotism.
"War, nostalgia, and nationalism, together with a contin-
gency plan to counter-balance American cultural influences, all created a potent melting pot into which folk music
was propelled," Michael Brocken has argued. Still, the links
between folk music in Britain and the United States were
clearly visible by war's end, and would only grow during
the following decades.

Similar forces were at work in the United States. The war
stimulated numerous antifascist, pro-war songs by Woody
Guthrie, Pete Seeger, and other activist folk musicians. The
members of the Almanac Singers struggled to keep performing into 1942, but soon became scattered. Pete Seeger
joined the Army, Woody Guthrie entered the Merchant
Marine, and others contributed their part to the war effort.
In 1943, however, Seeger, Butch and Bess Hawes, and Tom
Glazer recorded six Spanish Civil War songs for the Stin-
son/Asch label. The next year Seeger joined Glazer, Burl
Ives, Cisco Houston, Guthrie, and Josh White, under the
name Union Boys, to record the pro-war, pro-labor union
album *Songs for Victory*. Alan Lomax managed to produce two patriotic radio shows with folk dialog and songs
in 1944. *The Martins and the Coys*, using a hillbilly theme,
featured the stellar lineup of actor Will Geer, Ives, Sonny
Terry, Cisco Houston, Seeger, and country performers the
Coon Creek Girls and Wade Mainer. *The Chisholm Trail*,
with a western motif, included a similar cast. Oddly, both
shows were financed and recorded for the BBC, since no
domestic network would air the programs. Seeger, Guthrie, and many others also brought their music overseas,

making a strong connection with soldiers from throughout the country. By war's end folk music was poised to begin a rejuvenated life in a world free from fascism and, hopefully, war and poverty.

Grassroots folk musicians continued to perform for family and community through the war years. Others took their instruments, from the very portable harmonica to much more, as they traveled the world for war work, but would not leave their cherished music behind. Probably none were as well prepared as Woody Guthrie, however. His Merchant Marine colleague, Jim Longhi, described a scrawny Woody as they boarded their first ship in the spring of 1943: "We could barely see him under the load: a seabag over his shoulder, a guitar strapped to his back, a violin case, a mandolin case, a stack of at least ten books, and portable typewriter, all tied together by a length of clothesline and somehow wrapped around him."

POSTWAR YEARS

The postwar years in both the United Kingdom and the United States were both a continuation of prewar musical developments, and a slight prelude to the folk music revival that accelerated through the next decade. There was somewhat of an idealism following the victory over fascism that a new world was to emerge, where folk music could play a vital role. In Britain, "Regions of the country were enjoying folk song broadcasting of one form or another and, through embracing radio technology, folk music made several inroads in regions of the nation and national consciousness," according to Michael Brocken. He emphasizes the role of traditional singers, such as Harry Cox. Record companies and the BBC supplied country-dance music to the country, where teachers were encouraged to use traditional music in their classrooms. "The regularity with which British folk music appeared on the radio was indicative of the sense of loyalty to British culture and tradition felt at the BBC and among an educated middle-class audience." The EFDSS, with rising membership, sponsored its first commercial recordings of traditional performers, and expanded its musical classes, focusing on country dancing. Maud Karpeles, attempting to maintain her influential role in the organization and promote international cooperation, in 1947 convened a conference in London to form the International Folk Music Council.

Left-wing influence on folk music development in Britain was somewhat visible following the war, but not the presence it would take in the United States. A. L. Lloyd, following publication of *The Singing Englishman*, had slight public acknowledgment, although he did supply the songs for the BBC shows *Johnny Miner: A Ballad Opera for Coal* (1947) and *White Spirituals* (1949). Across the ocean, however, folk music and folk dancing had a wide following. In late December 1945 a gathering in Greenwich Village in New York City, called by Pete Seeger, launched People's Songs. Joined by Alan Lomax, Lee Hays, composer Earl Robinson, Woody Guthrie, and numerous others, the organization sought "to make and send songs of labor and the American people through the land." A published bulletin would print songs, new and old, as well as articles connecting music and activist politics throughout the country. Concerts, now named "hootenannies" (a musical event with various performers), records, publications such as a *People's Songs Wordbook* and *People's Song Book*, spread their musical messages, supporting world peace, labor unions, civil rights, and socialism. The organization tried to thrive in the face of a mounting cold war and anticommunist political atmosphere, as the United States and its allies feared the expansion of communism coming from Eastern Europe and the Soviet Union. Indeed, the fear increased after the Communist Party came into power in China in 1949. People's

Songs' successes were short-lived, and it collapsed in early 1949, but it left a lasting legacy.

While the left struggled to use folk music in various forms for political purposes, the genre was gaining a definite popular following and presence. There were numerous folk radio shows in New York City. Oscar Brand launched *Folk Song Festival* over WNYC in 1946 on Sunday evenings (still on the air in 2006); *Tom Glazer's Ballad Box* aired on ABC from 1945 to 1947; Elaine Lambert Lewis's *Folk Songs of the Seven Million* aired on WNYC starting in 1944. Alan Lomax resumed his radio career with his show *Your Ballad Man* on the Mutual Broadcasting Network. Rather than live performers, as he had on his prewar CBS shows, he now only played records, yet displaying his eclectic idea of folk music through including contemporary jazz and country performers. Not content to promote folk music only over the radio, he organized a biweekly series of concerts at Town Hall in New York, starting with "Blues at Midnight" in 1946, and including "Calypso at Midnight," "Spirituals at Midnight," and "Mountain Frolic at Midnight." He also produced various compilations for Decca Records, including Carl Sandburg's *Cowboy Songs and Negro Spirituals*, and albums by Burl Ives, Josh White, even actress Dorothy Lamour doing her favorite Hawaiian songs. His reissue albums *Listen to Our Story—A Panorama of American Ballads* and *Mountain Frolic* reissued recordings from the 1920s and 1930s by traditional performers Bradley Kincaid, Uncle Dave Macon, and Bascom Lamar Lunsford. While not the first to reissue hillbilly singers who were still alive—his father had put together *Smoky Mountain Ballads* for Victor Records in 1941, which included the Carter Family, Macon, and the Monroe Brothers—he was nonetheless a pioneer in recognizing the commercial contributions of country roots performers. Meanwhile, the Library of Congress was issuing a five-album set of his collected southern ballads, blues, and sacred songs. Indeed, Lomax hardly distinguished between

LEAD BELLY

Huddie "Lead Belly" Ledbetter can certainly be counted among the twentieth century's most outstanding and influential folk musicians. Born in Louisiana in 1888, he led a checkered career for some years, while learning to play the twelve-string guitar and concertina. He traveled briefly with the blues performer Blind Lemon Jefferson in Dallas, Texas, and soon after was convicted of murder and served almost seven years in a Texas state prison, being released in 1925 when pardoned by the governor. He continued his performing until 1930 when another crime sent him to prison in Angola, Louisiana, where he was recorded by John and Alan Lomax in 1933, as they traveled around the South for the Library of Congress. They again recorded him on a return visit in 1934, and soon after he was released and began working for John Lomax as his driver. He was not particularly a blues performer, but a powerful, eclectic musician who had a wide repertoire, including popular tunes. Some of his songs became influential, such as "Gray Goose," "Midnight Special," "Easy Rider," "C.C. Rider," and "Rock Island Line."

John Lomax brought him into the recording studio in New York in early 1935, where he recorded for the ARC label, which issued a few singles that sold poorly. He also recorded for the Library of Congress, and then Musicraft, which issued his first 78 album, *Negro Sinful Tunes*, in 1939. John and Alan Lomax had already published his musical autobiography, *Negro Folk Songs as Sung by Lead Belly* in 1936, when Lead Belly was getting much publicity, including a *Life* magazine feature in 1937. He had become involved with New York City's left-wing folk community, which included Aunt Molly Jackson, and soon Woody Guthrie and Pete Seeger. Victor issued *The Midnight Special and Other Prison Songs* in 1940, but his commercial appeal seemed weak, and so Lead Belly switched to Moses Asch's Asch label, which resulted in a series of albums, including *Work Songs of the U.S.A. Sung by Leadbelly*, *Play Party Songs Sung by Leadbelly*, and others on his subsequent Disc label. Lead Belly did most of his commercial recording for Asch, which would later be issued on his Folkways label.

Lead Belly's life and career during the 1940s, until his death in late 1949 from ALS (Lou Gehrig's disease), was not particularly successful, as he was bypassed by more commercial performers, such as Josh White and Burl Ives. He was mainly supported by his friends Pete Seeger, Woody Guthrie, Alan Lomax, and others on the political left. He also played for college students and at the Village Vanguard, a club in Greenwich Village, and even in Paris just before his death, but he had few commercial records by this time. In 1950 the Weavers had a major hit with Lead Belly's "Goodnight, Irene," and they also recorded his arrangement of "Kisses Sweeter Than Wine" and other songs, as did many others. A number of his songs, particularly "Rock Island Line," which became a hit for Lonnie Donegan in 1956, played a vital role in the skiffle craze in England.

By the folk revival of the 1960s Lead Belly had become an icon, his songs were widely known, and his recordings easily available on Folkways albums. In the 1990s Smithsonian Folkways would begin to issue a stream of CD compilations, including the three-disc *Lead Belly Legacy* series, and another covering *Lead Belly Sings for Children*, while Rounder Records released all of his original Library of Congress recordings for Alan Lomax. Other labels have also produced Lead Belly CDs, making his extensive output readily available. In 1988 he was inducted into the Rock and Roll Hall of Fame, along with the Beatles, the Beach Boys, and Woody Guthrie. As his biographers Charles Wolfe and Kip Lornell, in *The Life and Legacy of Leadbelly*, have well summarized his legacy: "Leadbelly was the first authentic traditional singer to go before the American people and make them aware of the rich vein of folk music that lay just beneath the surface of the hard bedrock of twentieth century industrial society. He also opened the door to the wonderous and potent world of African American folk culture and shared it with millions through the shaping power of his imagination." *Music Hound Folk: The Essential Album Guide* is more succinct (Walters and Mansfield 1998): "While he is recognized as a seminal blues artist, Leadbelly was also one of the greatest repositories of American folk music."

commercial and amateur performers in his quest to present folk music to a broader public. "Nineteen forty-six will be remembered, among other things, as the year that American folk songs came to town," he wrote in *Vogue*. And while "there may be an element of escapism in this trend," he cautioned in *The New York Times Magazine*, "the causes... lie deep in our national life: first, in our longing for artistic forms that reflect our democratic and equalitarian political beliefs; and, second, in our hankering after art that mirrors the unique life of this western continent."

Despite Lomax's somewhat utopian beliefs in the social power of folk music, however, most of the audience for folk music hardly considered its political or historic meanings, but just relished the simple melodies, straightforward stories, and familiar voices. The teenage Susan Reed, for example, quickly gained popularity. She was featured in *Life* magazine in late 1945: "Three times a night Café Society Uptown's choosy customers sit enraptured while Susie sings old Irish, English, Scottish, and Appalachian ballads and accompanies herself on the zither or the Irish Harp." She appeared frequently on NBC network shows, but also performed at Lunsford's Mountain Dance and Folk Festival in Asheville in 1948. Promoted as a simple mountain lass, she in fact had grown up in Chicago and Greenwich Village. Burl Ives became known not only as a popular folk singer but also as a movie actor. John Jacob Niles was born in Kentucky, performed southern mountain ballads in a high-pitch falsetto, recorded extensively, and published numerous songbooks. He developed a formal style, and appeared on concert stages rather than in folk festivals and on country music stations. Richard Dyer-Bennet was also a professional musician who resurrected ancient English ballads, played the guitar and lute, recorded extensively, and pursued a concert career. Josh White was a polished blues and pop singer who appeared at the fanciest night-clubs. Reed, Ives, Niles, Dyer-Bennet, and White were very popular through the 1940s and even after, indicating some of the commercial range of folk music at the time.

"There is no doubt that America in the last decade has begun to sing again," Courtlandt Canby noted in the *Saturday Review of Literature* in 1947. "Young people with a guitar singing together the cowboy ballads, or the songs of the Spanish Civil War, the *aficionados* of the ballad-singer cult, the more staid discovers of English folk songs, the blues devotees, the college and school glee clubs with their arrangements of songs from many lands—all have helped pull us out of the nineteenth-century slough of sentimentality and cheapness." Sheet music and songbooks spread folk songs throughout the country. The *Fireside Book of Folk Songs*, by Margaret Boni, was particularly popular.

Country music (still labeled "folk" in the *Billboard* and *Cashbox* magazine listings for a few more years) and the blues, while experiencing some changes, were aspects of folk music that had their own audiences and increasing popularity. Spade Cooley (king of Western Swing), Arthur Smith, Merle Travis, Ernest Tubb, Tex Ritter, the Sons of the Pioneers, Hank Williams, and Jack Guthrie (Woody's cousin), while exhibiting quite different styles, were some of the more popular country performers. Lester Flatt and Earl Scruggs joined Bill Monroe and the Blue Grass Boys in 1945, launching the new sound of bluegrass. The record companies responded accordingly. Hopping on the musical bandwagon, Capitol Records issued *Jo Stafford Sings American Folk Songs* in 1948, while crooner Bing Crosby's *Cowboy Songs* was only one of his "traditional" albums. Country music had weathered the war years and was prepared to attract a wide audience, particularly in the North (specifically California), where many southerners had moved, first fleeing the Depression and then attracted to war work. "In many respects the dawning period was to be the real 'golden age' of country music," historian Bill Malone has written. "Later decades would bring greater material rewards to country musicians, but no period would experience a happier fusion of 'traditional' sounds and commercial burgeoning than did the immediate postwar era." The Grand Ole Opry remained as popular as ever.

Blues musicians were still scattered around the South, in both rural and urban areas, playing mostly for family, friends, but also strangers in the proliferating road houses and juke joints. Some had moved North before the war, but their flight had accelerated, attracted (along with whites) to the availability of industrial jobs and a different cultural landscape (others joined the armed forces and discovered foreign lands and customs, often without racial discrimination). Particularly in Chicago, a different type of blues now emerged. Muddy Waters (born McKinley Morganfield), for instance, first recorded in rural Mississippi by Alan Lomax in 1941, moved to the Windy City in 1943, where he joined Big Bill Broonzy and other established blues men. Waters first recorded in 1946, but his distinctive electric guitar sound had to wait a few years to become established. By decade's end, however, joined by Little Walter, Howlin' Wolf, and numerous others, and promoted by the Chess brothers' record labels, Waters was leading a flashy urban blues renaissance that rippled throughout the country. In the South, for example, Memphis remained as an urban blues center.

The term rhythm and blues became associated with a related urban musical style emerging in this period. "Though not exclusive to the city, R & B was folk music that captured urban ethnic attitudes and mores," Barry Pearson has explained. "Successfully marketed to urban consumers (and rural folk who wished to be), R & B embodied the latest fads in language and dance; it spoke of heroes and even the consumer goods now within the reach of postwar blacks." The new sound was captured by Charles Brown, Joe Turner, Wynonie Harris, and particularly Louis Jordan. A spate of independent record companies, such as Chess, Atlantic, and Modern, fed the record stories and thousands of public jukeboxes with the revitalized sound. While the blues basically dealt with personal problems and issues, some songs dealt with the wider world of politics and foreign affairs. For example, at war's end there was Ivory Joe Hunter's "Reconversion Blues," Champion Jack Dupree's "God Bless Our New President" (Harry S. Truman), and Roosevelt Sykes's "High Price Blues." Some songs dealt with the atom bomb, such as Joe Houston's "Atom Bomb," Pete Johnson's "Atomic Boogie," and Slim Gaillard's "Atomic Cocktail." Race relations could also appear in a blues song, such as Big Bill Broonzy's "Black, Brown and White," while Lead Belly performed "Jim Crow Blues."

By decade's end folk music appeared in a variety of styles and sounds—traditional and contemporary, blues and country, gospel and rhythm and blues, ballads and work songs. Performers could be heard on concert stages, on front porches, on radio programs, on commercial recordings, at folk festivals, indeed just about everywhere. It was truly a part of the country's musical mix, and would only become more prominent in the near future. The same was true, but to a much lesser extent, in Great Britain, but this would soon change, as both countries experienced a folk boom that easily crossed the Atlantic.

4

THE FIFTIES

GREAT BRITAIN

Musical eras are seldom easily characterized by specific dates or decades, but in terms of the folk music revival, the year 1950 appears to have been an important turning point. There was, in particular, a much enhanced relationship between folk music and musicians in the United States and Great Britain, as both experienced an obvious revival, as well as a shaping and broadening of the vernacular musical landscape. By decade's end these influences and changes would be most visible, with significant results that would gain greater transformations in coming decades.

In September 1950, Maud Karpeles, who had worked with Cecil Sharp many decades earlier, returned to the United States at the behest of the Library of Congress. For over three weeks, accompanied by musicologist Sidney Robertson Cowell, she again visited the Appalachians, where she uncovered a few dozen singers, some of whom had been interviewed many years before. They managed to record almost 100 ballads and folk songs. The next year she summarized her trip in the *Journal of the English Folk Dance and Song Society*, where she lamented the arrival of technology, particularly the radio, "the arch-enemy, except in certain favored circumstances, of folk song." She remained the living link (or ghost) between song collectors past and present.

The English folk scene had various, even conflicting, aspects. The English Folk Dance and Song Society (EFDSS) continued its support for traditional songs and dances. While the society mostly tried to hold the line against modern influences, both A. L. "Bert" Lloyd and Ewan Mac-Coll expanded their reach and influence, particularly with the arrival of Alan Lomax. "The rise of the Second English Folk Revival has sometimes been dated from 1950, when Alan Lomax arrived in the U.K. looking for songs for the *World Library of Folk and Primitive Music*," Gerald Porter has noted. If this is not entirely true, it has much to be considered. As the anticommunist crusade heated up in the United States, with government loyalty oaths now imposed, and a cold war prevailing in international relations, Lomax decided to move to England in late 1950. The previous January he had organized a memorial concert for Lead Belly, who had died the previous month. Lomax featured his usual eclectic lineup, with Woody Guthrie, jazz greats Hot Lips Page and Sidney Bechet, Tom Glazer, calypso singer Lord Invader, W. C. Handy, traditional ballad singer Jean Ritchie, the Reverend Gary Davis, Sonny Terry and Brownie McGhee, and a new quartet, the Weavers. This attempt to demonstrate the wide spectrum of folk music would be Lomax's last fling in the United States for a decade. But in England he would use his tireless energy and artistic scope to shape and influence a creative, dynamic musical scene.

Lomax had a mix of reasons for moving to England, where he would establish his base until returning to the United States in 1958. Surely the mounting internal attack on communism was of major consideration, but he also had finished his book on the jazz pioneer Jelly Roll Morton, *Mr. Jelly Roll* (1950), and completed his radio series, "Your Ballad Man," for the Mutual Broadcasting System (1946–1949). He was now searching for broader horizons for his restless collecting spirit. He was struck by the mounting interest in studying the world's music, as indicated by the formation of the International Folk Music Council in 1946, and Moe Asch's founding of Folkways Records in 1949. Asch planned to issue records of the world's musical and oral traditions, which he would do for the next 40 years. The term "ethnomusicology" was coined in 1950, followed five years later by the formation of the Society for Ethnomusicology in the United States, in order to represent this interest in the world's vernacular musical styles. In the summer of 1950, just before his move to London, Lomax participated in the "Midcentury International Folklore Conference" at Indiana University. Following his advice to the conference participants to promote the exchange of recorded folk music between all of the world's countries, he signed an agreement with Columbia Records to issue a series of perhaps 30 LP records surveying this new field. He thought his stay in England would make possible "collaborating with the folk music experts of Europe and drawing upon their archives." He would be assisted by a Magnecord tape machine, the latest technology to ensure accurate field recordings.

After arriving in England, Lomax plunged into the developing folk scene. He first visited the Cecil Sharp House, where he met Douglas Kennedy, Director of the EFDSS. His son Peter, who had been collecting West Country folksingers, and Lomax became friends and collaborators. Lomax also now connected with Ewan MacColl and Bert Lloyd. MacColl (still using his given name Jimmie Miller) had been an actor who now turned to music for his artistic and political expression. Joined by Robin Roberts, an American actress and singer, Lomax started collecting in Ireland, obtaining the valuable cooperation of Seamus Ennis, who had a wealth of songs and played the uilleann pipes. Lomax had also begun his work for BBC in early 1951, first appearing on the *Traditional Ballads* show then immediately starting his own three-part series, *Adventure in Folk Song*, featuring himself and Roberts playing a range of American folk songs. A few months later he created three programs on *Patterns in American Folk Song*, also with Roberts, and followed with a series on *The Art of the Negro*, which included music from Big Bill Broonzy, Jelly Roll Morton, and many of his southern field recordings. "At

EWAN MACCOLL/PEGGY SEEGER

Ewan MacColl was born Jimmie Miller in Salford in 1915, the son of Scots parents who had moved to England in 1910. He early left school and took various working-class jobs while becoming self-educated at the Manchester Public Library. He wrote for factory newspapers and composed satirical songs before devoting his life to radical politics and theater. He married Joan Littlewood, a young actress, and they formed the Theatre of Action in Manchester, the first of a series of labor theaters into the early 1950s, although he had by now become divorced and married the dancer Jean Newlove. He had also switched to performing and promoting folk music, and in 1953 founded the Ballads and Blues Club (later the Singers Club) in London with Alan Lomax, A. L. Lloyd, and Seamus Ennis.

From the 1930s he had worked as an actor, narrator, writer, and producer on BBC radio, having been involved with various experimental programs. In 1956 he met Peggy Seeger and they collaborated on a series of musical documentaries, known as the *Radio-Ballads*, for BBC, for example *Song of a Road* on highway building, *Singing the Fishing* on the herring industry, and *The Big Hewer* on coal miners.

Peggy Seeger, born in 1935, was the daughter of musicologist Charles Seeger and composer Ruth Crawford Seeger, the sister of Mike Seeger, and the half-sister of Pete Seeger. A gifted musician on the piano, guitar, and banjo, with a once an enthusiastic championing of the music of ordinary black Americans and a damning indictment of Southern racism, *The Art of the Negro* was an extraordinarily powerful documentary feature that won Lomax many admirers and, no doubt, not a few enemies too," E. David Gregory has written. He was quickly establishing himself as a presence on BBC, which introduced its listeners to a wide range of folk music from across the Atlantic.

As Lomax worked with Peter Kennedy on the English volume for his Columbia Records series, the latter suggested he contact Lloyd and MacColl for industrial songs. Lloyd

rich folk music background, she first met MacColl on a trip to England in 1956, and they began living together in 1959. Peggy began recording folk albums in the 1950s, which she would continue into the next century. They had been part of a skiffle group, the Ramblers, along with Lomax, and in the 1960s began a series of albums together, including *The Long Harvest* (ten volumes), and *Blood and Roses* (five volumes), as well as recording numerous albums separately. They also kept up an active performing schedule, and composed many songs; MacColl's most popular, "The First Time I Ever Saw Your Face," written for Peggy, was a hit by Roberta Flack in 1971. *The Peggy Seeger Songbook: Warts and All: Forty Years of Songmaking* was published in 1998, and *The Essential Ewan MacColl Songbook: Sixty Years of Songmaking* three years later in 2001. They also recorded numerous traditional singers in Great Britain and published their songs in *Travellers' Songs of England and Scotland* and *Doomsday*.

MacColl died in 1989, and his *Journeymen: An Autobiography* was published the next year. Following Ewan's death, Peggy divided her time between living in the United States and England, and continued her busy performance schedule. MacColl and Seeger long combined their musical and political lives, creating a potent mix that has had great influence, although not without controversy. They also demonstrated the strong connections between folk music in Great Britain and the United States.

was working on his book *Come All Ye Bold Miners: Ballads and Songs of the Coalfields* (1952) and now found little time for Lomax, but MacColl was a different story. "My growing disenchantment with the theatre I had helped to build and my dissatisfaction with my work as a writer coincided with the arrival on the scene of Alan Lomax, an event which was to produce a major upheaval in my life," MacColl later recorded in his 1990 autobiography, *Journeyman*. Having met Lomax at BBC, MacColl came under the American's spell: "In the course of the next year or so I spent more and more time listening to Alan's enormous collection of tapes, to songs from the Americas, Africa, India, Italy, Spain and Britain, arguing, discussing, learning, and trying to acquire Alan's world-view of this extraordinary corpus of songs and stories.... Alan has amazing energy. Everything is done at breakneck speed." Lomax also got MacColl and Lloyd together for the first time, a fateful meeting.

Lomax, MacColl, and Lloyd were all involved in Communist party–related activities, which were more open in Great Britain than in the United States, for anticommunism was much less lethal in the former. Lomax, for example, took part in a musical tribute to Joe Vaughan, Communist mayor of Shoreditch, in 1951, where he joined MacColl in singing "One Big Union." Party members were involved in the first People's Festival Ceilidh in Scotland in 1951, which was associated with the simultaneous establishment of the School of Scottish Studies. Hamish Henderson's work with the school led to collecting songs from traditional singers Jeannie Robertson and the Stewart family of Blairgowrie. Meanwhile, in London, John Hasted, who taught Physics, began directing the London Youth Choir, formed by the London Labour Movement. Hasted was steeped in American labor/radical songs, particularly those by the Almanac Singers and Woody Guthrie, which helped shape his music and politics. He would play an active role in the British folk revival. Party members were involved in the first folk music festival, held in Sidmouth, Devon, in 1954. That same year party members Lesley and Harry Boardman launched Manchester's first folk club. "As in the United States, Party branches were beginning to seize on the power of progressive songs not only to build solidarity, but to make social, political meetings, and picket lines more lively," Gerald Porter has explained. Both traditional and new labor/radical songs were shared. Topic Records, launched by the Workers' Music Association in 1939, by the early 1950s, with Bert Lloyd as artistic director, was issuing an eclectic mix of radical music, some from Eastern Europe, classical as well as folk. Ewan MacColl performed workers songs and "The Ballad of Stalin," while Patrick Galvin did Irish tunes. MacColl and Lloyd also recorded albums of sailors' songs. Through contacts in the United States, particularly producer Kenneth Goldstein, American performers appeared on the Topic label and British singers were heard in the United States. Not all of these records had political/labor themes, such as Lloyd's anthology of industrial folksongs, *The Iron Muse* (1956), but left politics were influential in shaping the selections on both sides of the Atlantic. Topic would continue to issue records in England throughout the century.

In the early 1950s the folk revival began to accelerate, heading in various directions, with Lomax's steady involvement. Beginning with recording English and Irish traditional performers, he next moved to Scotland, where he secured the help of Hamish Henderson and William Montgomerie. Lomax's collections were part of two BBC programs, *I Heard Scotland Sing*, soon followed by *The Gaelic West*, which demonstrated to a broader British audience that Gaelic folk songs were alive and well. For six months in 1952 he traveled through Spain, then returned to Britain to record Harry Cox, Jeannie Robertson, and other traditional singers. He also worked with Lloyd, MacColl, Isla Cameron, and jazzman Humphrey Lyttleton on the series *Ballads and Blues*. Similar to his earlier radio programs in the United States, although MacColl now did most of the research and scripting, each show had a particular theme, such as "The Singing Sailormen," "Song of the Iron Road," and "The Hammer and the Loom." Older British folk songs were compared and contrasted with American folk, jazz, and blues lyrics. "In 1953 MacColl's vision of the revival," E. David Gregory has explained, "like Lomax's, was of an eclectic music of working people that would naturally mix songs and tunes from both sides of the Atlantic."

Indeed, in the 1950s Britain increasingly served as a magnet for various American performers. Blues men were somewhat familiar through their recordings and war-time radio broadcasts, so the burgeoning jazz community warmly greeted Josh White's arrival in 1950, part of his European tour (the previous year Lead Belly had performed in Paris, but not in the U.K.). Big Bill Broonzy's trip to England in 1951 was, therefore, rather exceptional. A recording of the singer Lomax made in 1947 was part of *The Art of the Negro* program, but Broonzy appeared live on *Song of the Iron Road*, (broadcast in November 1952), performing "John Henry" and "the Midnight Special." He had already performed and recorded in England the previous year, but returned in early 1952, and again later that year for his third visit, when he was joined by gospel diva Mahalia Jackson for two concerts (he also toured in 1955 and 1957).

Traditional ballad singer and mountain dulcimer player Jean Ritchie, accompanied by her photographer husband George Pickow, also arrived in 1952. She was born in Viper, Kentucky in 1922—not long after Cecil Sharp had visited the Hindman Settlement School, where he had collected songs from her family, including "Fair Nottamun Town" and "The Farmer's Cursed Wife"—and in 1947, following college, she moved to New York City and first met Lomax. Curious about her British folk roots, she obtained a Ful-bright Scholarship from the U.S. government and crossed the Atlantic. She first appeared on one of the *Ballads and Blues* programs, then traveled with Lomax and Peter Kennedy on a collecting trip to Devon and Cornwall. She collected traditional singers in Scotland and Ireland, recording Seamus Ennis, Tommy Makem, and numerous others. Oddly, Ritchie, as well as popular folksinger Burl Ives, briefly had their own BBC programs, thanks to Lomax's connections. Ritchie and Pickow soon returned to the United States.

By mid-decade the British airwaves seemed to be rich with both British and American folk song programs. MacColl had shows on British industrial songs, topical songs, and traditional ballads stretching into 1953. Peter Kennedy and Lomax designed the long-running series *As I Roved Out*, lasting from 1953 to 1958 and using discussions and field recordings made by Kennedy, Ennis, and others about rural life. Lomax also initiated a BBC television series in 1953, *Song Hunger: Alan Lomax*, in which he discussed his collecting trips in England and Spain; he also played these field recordings on separate BBC radio shows. The programs featured numerous British performers, including MacColl, Isla Cameron, Ennis, Margaret Barry, Harry Cox, and the Copper family, as well as the newcomer Theodore Bikel. Born in Vienna, Bikel had lived in Israel before moving to London (and finally the United States in 1954). Bikel was a talented actor and singer, performing in many languages. He met Lomax in London, who introduced him to the Irish Gypsy singer Margaret Barry. "She played an old beat-up banjo in a sort of flamenco style and I thought she was simply wonderful," he would write in his autobiography. "Lomax certainly deserves credit for creating the first television series in the U.K. in which source singers and traditional folk songs were featured front and centre," E. David Gregory has written.

SKIFFLE

The British folk scene was thriving by midcentury, fueled by a mix of traditional and modern singers, mostly from Britain and the United States. Through the promotional energies of Alan Lomax, Ewan MacColl, and Peter Kennedy there were numerous performances on BBC radio and television, as well as on concert stages. Much of this musical combination came together in the form of skiffle music, an odd British hybrid that captured public attention for a few years. American jazz had come to England in earlier decades, but became particularly popular following World War II; traditional (or trad) jazz, based on the "original" New Orleans style, had developed a strong following. The term skiffle had been used in the United States in the 1920s as another term for a house party with jazz, and in 1925 there was a Chicago Skiffle jazz group; a few years later Paramount Records issued a sampler *Hometown Skiffle* record, with Blind Blake, Blind Lemon Jefferson, and others. Bands led by Ken Colyer and Chris Barber, with Lonnie Donegan the banjo player first with Colyer then Barber, led the way. In 1952 Ken Colyer's Jazzmen formed an offshoot, which his brother Bill suggested should be called a skiffle group. They were influenced by the songs and stylings of Josh White, Big Bill Broonzy, blues man Lonnie Johnson, Lead Belly, Burl Ives, and Woody Guthrie. It took a few more years for the sound to catch on. In April 1957 a large concert was held at Royal Festival Hall, billed as "London's First Big Skiffle Session." Leading the way were Colyer, Alexis Korner, Chas McDevitt, and Donegan. McDevitt has written that at "one point in 1957, it was estimated that there were between 30,000 and 50,000 groups in the British Isles. The sale of guitars was booming and it was reported that more music shops than jewellers were being broken into." Skiffle clubs quickly opened, and skiffle records were very popular. The Chris Barber Jazz Band, with Donegan, in 1954 had recorded the album *New Orleans Joys*, which included the songs "Rock Island Line" and "John Henry." In 1956 the single of "Rock Island Line" was very successful in both Britain and the United States, leading to Donegan quickly becoming a major recording star. For the next few years skiffle dominated the music charts, with Donegan alone having 30 hit records. BBC radio launched the *Saturday Skiffle Club*, which lasted for 61 weeks.

Skiffle's appeal was broad indeed. Alan Lomax and Ewan MacColl joined the bandwagon. Together they created the Ramblers, with Shirley Collins, Peggy Seeger, Pete's half-sister and newly arrived from the United States, and others. They issued one album, *Alan Lomax and the Ramblers*, in 1956, They also made 14 one-hour programs for Granada TV. Lomax considered skiffle to be a healthy musical movement, since it would hopefully lead to a greater interest in traditional British songs. "Now it is noticeable that the skifflers are beginning to show interest in other songs than jailhouse ditties and bad man ballads," he wrote in 1957. "I have the greatest confidence in the world that their mastery of their instruments will increase, that they will get tired after a while of their monotonous two-beat imitation of Negro rhythm and that, in looking around, they will discover the song-tradition of Great Britain. This tradition, in melodic terms, is probably the richest in Western Europe." Initially based in youth clubs and coffee bars, dance halls and theaters, skiffle reached a broader audience in 1957 with the launching of the BBC TV program *Six-Five Special*, which featured live groups. The Skiffle Cellar now opened in London, featuring the top skiffle and jazz bands, as well as Americans Jack Elliott and Derrol Adams, Peggy Seeger, and Sonny Terry and Brownie McGhee. The Chas McDevitt Skiffle Group traveled to the United States in 1957 and even appeared on the popular Ed Sullivan TV show. Lonnie Donegan, however, was the most popular performer on both sides of the Atlantic. Unlike rock and roll, which had an aura of rebellion, skiffle was considered safe by the establishment. Indeed, Brian Bird, author of *Skiffle: The Story of Folk Song with a Jazz Beat* (1958), was a country clergyman who believed that "Skiffle has achieved a genuine social significance, and Skifflers have become the purveyors of the people's music in all its glory." He thought skiffle had an assured future, but this was not to be; its popularity waned by 1958. "Skiffle's life was short but it was, without doubt, the foundation upon which the next two decades of British popular music was built," concludes historian Michael Brocken. Some skiffle musicians continued to perform folk music, while many others preferred rock and roll. "With this hybrid of African-American blues, Anglo-American folk, and traditional jazz, many British performers and audiences were apparently also exposed to a range of traditional American and British material for the first time," ethnomusicologist Britta Sweers has concluded.

LOMAX, MACCOLL, AND LLOYD

While Lomax and MacColl had become involved with skiffle, they were more interested in pursuing other, more traditional, music projects. Lomax, for example, continued to work on the *Columbia World Library* record series, issuing 14 LPs in 1955, with more to come. He also worked with Peter Kennedy on ten volumes of *The Folksongs of Britain*, based on field recordings, which finally appeared on the Caedmon label in the early 1960s. Some of his recordings from the United States, Spain, and Italy were incorporated in his short-lived BBC radio program *Memories of a Ballad Hunter* in early 1957, and the next year he launched *A Ballad Hunter Looks at Britain*. The latter included songs collected throughout the British Isles. He would soon return to the United States.

Lloyd and MacColl began to record LP records, starting with *The Singing Sailor* for Topic in 1955. Finding it difficult to release much more in the U.K., with Lomax's assistance they found a ready audience in the United States. As a start they recorded nine albums of *The English and Scottish Popular Ballads (The Child Ballads)* and *Great British Ballads Not Included in the Child Collections* for Riverside Records in 1956. Kenneth Goldstein, a record producer for Riverside, was anxious to introduce the American market to British traditional ballads. Along with Lloyd and Seamus Ennis, MacColl began performing at the Ballads and Blues Club in London in 1954, launching the folk club movement. "While the greater part of our programmes consisted of the kind of songs which even the most strict traditionalists would class as folk material, that is, country songs, versions of the English and Scots popular ballads, sea shanties and forebitters," MacColl has written, "we were also attempting to extend the national repertory by introducing children's street songs, industrial songs and ballads, epigrammatic squibs, popular melodies, broadside ballads and new songs written in the folk idiom." His eclectic approach captured the expansive nature of the unfolding folk song movement. Folk clubs soon sprouted throughout the country. The Edinburgh University Folk Song Society started in 1958, followed the next year by one at Glasgow University; they were the beginnings of a proliferating movement in Scotland that expanded through the 1960s.

Eric Winter and John Hasted launched a national folk magazine, *Sing,* in 1954, focusing on topical songs that promoted peace, international fellowship, and workers' rights. The third issue, for example, included Ewan MacColl's "Ballad of Ho Chi Minh," which praised the leader of the rebellion in Vietnam against the French occupation. Labor songs, old and new, were well represented, including many from the United States. Some associated with the magazine, including editor Winter, Bert Lloyd, and Fred Dallas, were also members of the more traditional EFDSS, who were attempting to create a broad folk music movement. Their agenda, heavily political and present-oriented, differed somewhat from the society's leading members, such as Peter Kennedy, who preferred the more traditional songs and singers.

Peggy Seeger, daughter of musicologist Charles Seeger and composer Ruth Crawford Seeger, and half-sister of Pete, first arrived in England in 1956, when she met Ewan MacColl. An accomplished banjo and piano player, steeped in traditional songs and ballads, she returned in 1958 and married MacColl the following year. She next learned to play the autoharp, concertina, and dulcimer, began to write songs, and would record numerous albums with MacColl. She would live in England until MacColl's death in 1989, serving as a vital link between the British and American folk song communities. But she was certainly not alone.

Jack Elliott, born Elliott Adnopoz in Brooklyn, New York, in 1931, the son of a doctor, early in life decided to become a cowboy. He learned to play the guitar and wound up meeting Woody Guthrie in early 1951, who became his friend and musical role model. Jack arrived in London in 1955 and soon connected with Alan Lomax, who gave him a role in his BBC production *The Big Rock Candy Mountain*; and with Lomax's help he quickly recorded for Topic Records, first an album entitled *Woody Guthrie's Blues* then various singles. He briefly joined a skiffle group, The City Ramblers, but preferred to accompany his old friend from Portland, Oregon, Derroll Adams, who had also arrived in London. With Jack on the guitar and Derroll on the banjo they made the rounds of the skiffle clubs, the Blue Angel, a fancy nightclub, and even performed for Princess Margaret. They also recorded for Topic and appeared on various radio programs. "Imagine the impact that these two urban cowboys must have had on me in 1958," budding musician Jeff Cloves later explained. "[T]hey both wore Levis, high-heeled, tooled cowboy boots and stetsons." Ramblin' Jack Elliott, as he was now known, returned to the United States in early 1961. Along with Peggy Seeger, he was particularly influential on the style of many British folk performers. Cloves, who first saw Elliott at the Round House in London, later testified that he was "the greatest club entertainer I have ever seen."

While *Sing* magazine covered folk happenings in the United States, *Caravan*, a folk magazine published in Greenwich Village beginning in 1957, for a brief time was keen to follow events across the Atlantic, further connecting the two folk scenes. In early 1958 Sandy Paton, a young musician just arrived in London from the United States, reported in *Caravan* that he attended a party at Alan Lomax's with another American, Guy Carawan, as well as Peter Kennedy, Shirley Collins, and Seamus Ennis. "Shirley does a lot of American material and does it well, but we think she really stands out when she does the English ballads of her own folk tradition," Paton concluded. In May 1957 John Brunner reported that Sonny Terry and Brownie McGhee have been touring with the Chris Barber skiffle band. During Carawan's brief stay he also met MacColl, Lloyd, and even Maud Karpeles at the EFDSS's Cecil Sharp House. The close ties across the Atlantic would only grow in the following decade.

THE UNITED STATES

Lead Belly died in Bellevue Hospital on December 6, 1949, a victim of the debilitating ALS. While his career had not particularly flourished following the war, he had continued to give concerts and make records. His musical legacy would expand over the coming decades. But Lead Belly's death was not the only significant event at decade's end. In late August 1949 People's Artists, the successor to the left-wing People's Songs, had planned a concert with Paul Robeson and Pete Seeger to be held in Peekskill, New York, just north of New York City. An anticommunist mob rioted, preventing the concert from occurring, but a second concert with Robeson and Seeger did take place on September 4. While the performers were protected during the concert, as the crowd was leaving they were stoned by the angry mob, resulting in numerous casualties. This indication of mounting Cold War hysteria was a cruel blow to those who thought a peaceful world might be possible.

While the Cold War was escalating, at the end of 1949 four members of People's Songs, Pete Seeger, Ronnie Gilbert, Lee Hays, and Fred Hellerman, who had been informally performing together, began a limited engagement at the Village Vanguard nightclub in Greenwich Village. Using the name "The Weavers," they initially attracted

PETE SEEGER

Pete Seeger has been the most influential figure in promoting and influencing popular folk music in the United States since the 1930s. Born in New York City in 1919, his rich musical background came from his father, Charles, a classical music scholar and composer, and later an ethnomusicologist, and his mother, Constance, a violinist and teacher. Pete attended private schools and briefly Harvard College before launching out on his own. After attending Bascom Lamar Lunsford's music festival in Asheville, North Carolina, in 1935, he developed his love for the five-string banjo. For about one year he served as Alan Lomax's assistant at the Archive of Folk Song at the Library of Congress, and soon after met Woody Guthrie, with whom he traveled around the country. Back in New York in 1941 he formed the Almanac Singers with Lee Hays and Millard Lampell. Soon joined by various others, including Sis Cunningham, Bess Lomax (Alan's sister), Pete and Butch Hawes, and even Guthrie, they performed at labor rallies and recorded a few albums of topical and traditional folk songs, including the influential *Talking Union and Other Union Songs*.

Pete served in the Army during World War II, and following the war he helped launch People's Songs, an organization designed to promote topical songs. People's Songs collapsed in 1949, but quickly Pete joined Lee Hays, Ronnie Gilbert, and Fred Hellerman in the Weavers, who had a series of popular song hits, starting with Lead Belly's "Goodnight Irene" in 1950. The Weavers's successful career was cut short in 1953 because of the developing anticommunist crusade, although the Weavers regrouped in late 1955 and Pete remained with them for a few more years. His recording career had begun in 1941, and in addition to his recordings with the Weavers, he produced a large number of albums for Moe Asch's Folkways label throughout the 1950s.

Pete switched to Columbia Records in the 1960s, and recorded many popular albums, as well as composing numerous popular folk songs, including "The Hammer Song" (with Lee Hays), "Turn, Turn, Turn" (a hit for the Byrds in 1965), and "Where Have All the Flowers Gone." He also continued a hectic performing schedule, first at schools, and increasingly at folk festivals and in concert halls through the 1960s. He had first self-published his banjo instruction manual in 1948, which soon became the starting point for all subsequent banjo players, and he also recorded a guitar instruction album.

He had long supported world peace, civil rights, and labor unions, and in the late 1960s he became an environmental activist with initiating the sloop *Clearwater* in order to publicize cleaning up the polluted Hudson River. He also published a number of books, including *Where Have All the Flowers Gone*, filled with 200 of his songs. Honored by the Kennedy Center in Washington, D.C. and inducted into the Rock and Roll Hall of Fame, he continued his active schedule into the twenty-first century, when he was well into his eighties. Through a busy career, marked by numerous highs and lows, Seeger never faltered and has been considered the most consistent and important influence on shaping the modern folk music movement. His albums, perhaps totaling close to 100, are still generally available, particularly through Smithsonian Folkways Recordings; he received a Grammy Award in 1997 for the album *Pete*. His numerous compositions have been recorded by Bonnie Raitt, Roger McGuinn, Richie Havens, and other contemporary artists on a series of CDs issued by Appleseed Recordings: *Where Have All the Flowers Gone: The Songs of Pete Seeger* (1998), *The Songs of Pete Seeger: If I Had a Song* (2001), and *Seeds: The Songs of Pete Seeger* (2003).

little attention, but by the end of their extended six-month stay they were getting rave reviews and a record contract with Decca. This was the start of a Cinderella story that was all too brief, but certainly indicated the potential for folk music to reach a broad, enthusiastic public. Their recording of the single "Tzena, Tzena"/"Goodnight, Irene" hit a popular nerve. The Israeli tune shot up the popular record charts in midsummer, reaching number three. The Lead Belly song "Goodnight, Irene" made it to number one, and remained popular for 25 weeks. The Weavers followed with a string of other hits, including "The Roving Kind," the Woody Guthrie song, "So Long (It's Been Good to Know Yuh)," "On Top of Old Smoky," "Wimoweh," a South African song adapted by Seeger, and Lead Belly's "Midnight Special." "Songs like ours getting on the Hit Parade broke down the barriers between country and pop," Lee Hays argued. While the Weavers expressed no overt radical politics in their music, their selection of African-American songs and those from other countries certainly hinted at their commitment to civil rights and international understanding and cooperation. Many of their hits were covered by others, such as popular singers Frank Sinatra and Jo Stafford, and their lush melodies with big band backing were a far cry from the rustic, acoustic sources of many of their songs. While this could not be considered traditional folk music, their repertoire was based on a wide range of folk materials and certainly possessed a folk sensibility.

The Weavers's influence would reach across the following two decades, for they would serve as the inspiration and prototype for the plethora of folk trios, quartets, and so many more that would soon spring up, but their initial career was cut short by the gathering forces of anti-communism. By 1953 they were no longer recording or performing. Other folk musicians also had their careers curtailed, if not crushed, by the Red Scare. Paul Robeson lost his passport, crippling his career for some years. Burl

Ives, on the other hand, informed on a couple of his old friends, including Richard Dyer-Bennet, in his testimony before the House Un-American Activities Committee. Josh White was forced to denounce his former political affiliations before the same committee, although he did not name any names of former "communists." The anti-communist climate certainly threatened to destroy popular folk performers, but its harsh effect was of limited duration. Indeed, the Weavers regrouped in late 1955, at a famous Christmas concert at Carnegie Hall, and continued to perform for many years. Coincidentally, in 1953 John Greenway published *American Folk Songs of Protest*, the first scholarly study of the country's left-wing musical legacy, a rich collection of workers, farmers, and radical songs just as the red scare was reaching its height.

FOLK SONG SCHOLARSHIP

Folk music scholarship continued through the decade, further documenting the range and depth of the country's traditional ballads and songs. Malcolm Laws published *Native American Balladry* in 1950, a broad survey of the topic, with a subsequent volume, *American Balladry From British Broadsides*, appearing seven years later. Tristram Coffin's *The British Traditional Ballad in North America* (1950) also denoted the continuing academic interest in the ballad style, while Vance Randolph focused more on common folk songs in his four-volume compilation of *Ozark Folksongs* (1946–1950), part of his broad interest in vernacular music and stories from Arkansas and Missouri. One sympathetic critic marveled that Randolph could find such treasures where, "according to legend, shoeless natives chase razorback hogs, or spend their time drinking moonshine whisky under the trees." Laws, Coffin, Randolph, and other collectors continued the longstanding search for folk songs and ballads, which would fuel the oncoming folk music revival.

A significant influence on the developing folk music scene was increasing access to the expanding world of both written and recorded folk styles, whether deriving from ancient or modern sources. For example, in 1952 Moe Asch's Folkways Records issued what would become a most influential three-volume six-record set, known as the *Anthology of American Folk Music*. Compiled by Harry Smith from his own collection of 78 rpm records of black and white roots musicians from the 1920s and 1930s, the set would quickly take on a life of its own. An eccentric character and amateur anthropologist, Smith introduced a new audience to the music of the Carter Family, Buell Kazee, Clarence Ashley, Furry Lewis, Mississippi John Hurt, and Blind Lemon Jefferson. While they might have seemed like relics from some distant past, and most of the original records were indeed very difficult to locate, in fact these recordings were only a few decades old and many of the performers were still alive (only to be rediscovered within a few years). "That set became our bible," Dave Van Ronk has written. "It is how most of us first heard Blind Willie Johnson, Mississippi John Hurt, and even Blind Lemon Jefferson. And it was not just blues people, by any means. It had ballad singers, square-dance fiddling, gospel congregations." When the *Anthology* was reissued by Smithsonian/ Folkways Records in 1997 in an elaborate CD box, to great sales and acclaim, many critics praised Smith's selections of commercial recordings while downplaying the value of the field recordings of John and Alan Lomax, with the former considered a truer expression of America's folk heritage.

John Lomax, however, was the first to reissue early commercial records by the Carter Family, Uncle Dave Macon, the Monroe Brothers, and others in the album *Smoky Mountain Ballads* for Victor in 1941. Alan Lomax, most known for his field recordings, initially for the Library of Congress, also compiled two albums of earlier hillbilly records, *Listen to Our Story—A Panorama of American*

Ballads and *Mountain Frolic* on the Brunswick label in 1947. He included Bradley Kincaid, Bascom Lamar Lunsford, Buell Kazee, among others. Both Lomaxes included mostly recordings from white performers—Alan's *Listen to Our Story* did contain, however, Furry Lewis's "Stackolee" and the Reverend Edward Clayborn's "True Religion"—while Harry Smith had more of a racial and ethnic mix. On his Mutual Broadcasting radio show in the late 1940s, moreover, Alan Lomax had played records from a wide variety of folk, blues, gospel, and country performers.

There was a fine line between field and commercial recordings at the time, with both supplying a rich legacy of music for the growing folk music audience. Folkways Records, in addition to issuing the Smith *Anthology*, also poured forth an unending stream of field recordings from the United States and throughout the world in the 1950s. For example, Asch would release southern field recordings by Harold Courlander, *Negro Folk Music U.S.A.* in 1963, and also Frederic Ramsey, whose work appeared in *Music from the South*. Both Courlander and Ramsey demonstrated that a variety of vernacular black musical styles, including blues and gospel, secular and religious, were alive and well in the 1950s. Later in the decade folklorist Harry Oster in Louisiana, Mack McCormick in Texas, and Sam Charters were also discovering a wealth of southern blues talent, including Sam "Lightnin'" Hopkins. Oster followed in the footsteps of the Lomaxes by visiting the Louisiana State Penitentiary in 1959 and recording Robert Pete Williams, among others.

When Alan Lomax returned to the United States in 1958 he lost no time in also revisiting the South to continue his field recordings, starting in Virginia, traveling through Tennessee and Mississippi, including the infamous Parchman prison farm, and winding up in the Georgia Sea Islands. He was now accompanied by Shirley Collins, who had done field work with Lomax in England and also helped with his *The Folk Songs of North America*, a large and influential book published in 1960. She joined Alan in New York in early 1959, and after attending the Berkeley and Newport folk festivals they headed south. They recorded traditional singers Texas Gladden, her brother Hobart Smith, banjo player Wade Ward, the Memphis Jug Band, the Sacred Harp Singers in Alabama, ballad singer Almeda Riddle, and numerous others. She returned to England at year's end. "I missed Alan dreadfully," she has written in her autobiography *America Over the Water* (2004), "but I was young and resilient and picked up the threads in England again. The Folk Revival was getting under way, folk clubs flourishing all over the country, and I was able to make a living as a singer." There was a great social and cultural distance between London in 1960 and the southern backwaters, but through folk music they could be bridged by Collins, Lomax, and countless others.

MID-DECADE MUSIC

By the midfifties there was a broad mixture of popular musical styles available in concerts and on records, radio programs, and even some television stations. While rock and roll, particularly with the appearance of Elvis Presley in 1954 on Sun Records, was capturing the attention of an escalating population of young consumers (although the bulk of the baby boom generation would not reach adolescence until the next decade). Youth oriented magazines and clothing styles, as well as the appearance of the cheap, unbreakable vinyl 45-rpm record by 1950, all fueled the growing market. The rock and roll of Presley, Little Richard, Chuck Berry, however, still shared the market with the crooning of Bing Crosby, Perry Como, the Ink Spots, Rosemary Clooney, and other pop singers.

There were also other musical styles trying to compete, with some success. Chess Records in Chicago, Sun Records in Memphis, Atlantic Records in New York, Savoy Records in Newark, New Jersey, Vee-Jay Records in Gary, Indiana, and countless other small labels were issuing a steady stream of rhythm and blues records. Rhythm and blues, a term that replaced the former race records designation, appeared following World War II. "Though not exclusive to the city, R & B was folk music that captured urban ethnic attitudes and mores," music historian Barry Pearson has explained. "Successfully marketed to urban consumers (and rural folk who wished to be), R & B embodied the latest fads in language and dance; it spoke of heroes and even the consumer goods now within the reach of postwar blacks—automobiles, clothing, popular beverages. An index of African-American popular culture, R & B presaged a consumer mentality concerned with this week's current hits, in contrast to the popular music of the 1920s and 1930s, when a record might sell for five years or more." Among the performers were Ruth Brown, Clyde McPhatter, Arthur "Big Boy" Crudup, Litter Walter Jacobs, Jimmy Reed, and Muddy Waters. Aimed at black consumers, the record companies soon discovered a growing white audience. "By 1955, rhythm and blues was in full bloom, inexorably expanding into the popular market," Pearson concludes, although now the broader label rock and roll would replace the R & B designation. The latter term would encompass a broad range of performers, from Fats Domino to Pat Boone, both black and white.

While R & B was capturing a growing segment of the youth market, country music also demonstrated a national appeal. During his short professional career (1947–1953), Hank Williams attracted a wide audience that was further explored by other performers. Many labels, such as Sun, issued recordings by both country and R & B performers. Country radio programs, such as the *Grand Ole Opry* out of Nashville and the *Louisiana Hayride* from Shreveport, Louisiana, reached a nationwide audience, including youngsters in northern cities who were searching for something different from the current pop tunes. But the musical scene was rapidly changing. Country performers such as Bill Haley and Elvis Presley moved over to rockabilly by mid-decade, an upbeat sound that combined country blues with honky-tonk country and heavy guitar effects. "As country blues [was] intended for young urbanites, rockabilly disavowed middle-class respectability in favor of primal debauchery," country historian Jeffrey Lange has argued. "In doing so, it reached a generation of Americans coming of age in the postwar era." It also generated a sizeable backlash from adults who feared that rockabilly and rock and roll, with African-American overtones, would increase sexual behavior and weaken the country's moral fiber. Glenn Altschuler has tried to capture the complexities of the musical fifties in his study, *All Shook Up* (2003): "Rock 'n' roll deepened the divide between the generations, helped teenagers differentiate themselves from others, transformed popular culture in the United States, and rattled the reticent by pushing sexuality into the public arena. Anything but a 'great unifying force,' rock 'n' roll kept many Americans in the 1950s off balance, on guard, and uncertain about their families and the future of their country."

FOLK MUSIC AT MID-DECADE

Historians of rock and roll, and popular music more broadly, in the fifties usually overlooked the growing popularity of folk music. But it was certainly part of the musical mix of the time, with performers appearing in concerts and festivals, on records and radio, and even somewhat on television. "Folk songs are the articulated expression of the experience of a people (a nation)," popular actor and singer Burl Ives argued in *Variety*, the show business newspaper, in 1955. "These songs are a shared heritage, and when the people of a country can sing of these things together, it can only strengthen their national bonds." While Ives was making a case for the patriotic nature of folk music, in order to counter its left-wing tinge, at the same time a foreign import briefly caught the public's imagination. Calypso originated among former slaves and Creoles in Port of Spain, Trinidad, in the West Indies, as part of Carnival celebrations in the nineteenth century. Singers such as Atilla the Hun, the Roaring Lion, and Lord Invader became popular performers in the United States in the twentieth century, conveying news and telling stories through the calypso style. In 1944 the popular Andrews Sisters had a surprise hit with "Rum and Coca-Cola," a calypso written by Lord Invader. By the early 1950s calypso singers were particularly popular in New York City. But it was Harry Belafonte who made calypso a temporary phenomenon, and in the process launched a musical career that would continue into the twenty-first century.

Born in New York in 1927, Belafonte spent part of his childhood in his mother's native Jamaica. He finished school in New York, served in the Navy during World War II, and his singing career began to take off in the early 1950s. Specializing in folk songs, his first album, *"Mark Twain" and Other Folk Favorites* appeared in 1954. But it was the album *Calypso*, released in 1956, that included "Day-O" (aka "The Banana Boat Song"), "Jamaica Farewell," and "Man Smart," which ignited the calypso craze and Belafonte as the King of Calypso. The album sold over a million and a half copies, an extravagant number at the time, while the single of "Day-O" remained on the pop charts for 20 weeks. Curiously, the Tarriers, an interracial trio, also had a hit with "The Banana Boat Song" just before Belafonte's version, and it was recorded as well by Sarah Vaughn, the Fontaine Sisters, and other pop acts. But Belafonte's version would stimulate the short-lived calypso fad, despite the singer's attempts to broaden his appeal. "The present hysterical type of fervor for any melodies that even remotely resemble Calypso will wear out and drive it to premature obscurity," Belafonte stated in early 1957. He was correct, although for a brief moment a spate of calypso magazines and movies fueled a market somewhat driven by an attempt to counter the growing popularity of rock and roll. Indeed, the magazine *Elvis vs. Belafonte* tried to exploit the contrived "Big Battle of 1957—Rock 'n' Roll vs. Calypso." But calypso faded about as quickly as it had appeared, although yet another indication that folk music could generate a large audience if it is unique and packaged well. Calypso somewhat paralleled skiffle in its short-lived attraction, while reaching out to a new audience for folk music.

By mid-decade the folk music scene was particularly heating up in New York City, but it was also becoming more apparent in many other northern urban and college communities. Folklorist Norm Cohen has attempted to account for this upsurge in popularity in his broad study, *Folk Music: A Regional Exploration*. Popular music "had become particularly bland musically and insipid lyrically," he argues, and because folk music was based "on easy-to-learn instruments like the guitar and banjo, it invited listeners to learn to play and sing the songs themselves." Moreover, artists "like the Weavers and Harry Belafonte were enormously dynamic and appealing: the former to those who liked their entertainment tinged with politics, and the latter to those who didn't."

A core group of performers lived in New York City, where many gathered on Sunday afternoons during the summer in Greenwich Village's Washington Square Park. "The Washington Square Sunday afternoon scene was a great catalyst for my whole generation," Dave Van Ronk recalls. "It kept getting bigger and bigger every year, and by the late 1950s it had become a tourist attraction as well." Some would be playing bluegrass music, other singing songs from Israel or the Old Left, others playing blues or old-time ballads, indicating the broad reach of folk music at the time. Even Woody Guthrie would be brought to the Square when possible from the New Jersey State Hospital at Greystone Park, where he was permanently hospitalized in 1956 suffering from Huntington's disease. The folk magazine *Sing Out!*, launched in 1950 with an office in New York, limped through the decade, but kept the flame alive for those who desired new songs and information on performers and folk activities. In 1959 Israel G. Young, who had recently opened the Folklore Center in Greenwich Village, initiated his "Frets and Frails" column in *Sing Out!*, which connected readers throughout the country to the comings and goings of performers and so many others for the next decade. Young sold records, songbooks, magazines, and instruments at the Folklore Center, opened in early 1957, and generally functioned as a convenient gathering place for musicians and fans until its closing in 1973. "When Izzy opened that little hole," Van Ronk explains, "there was suddenly a place where everyone went, and it became a catalyst for all sorts of things." He also arranged concerts, either in his store or elsewhere, and generally served as not just the local but the national folk central. Soon folklore centers were springing up around the country.

The Café Bizarre opened in the Village in mid-1957, the first local folk music coffeehouse. Professional performers had long appeared at the Village Vanguard and earlier at Café Society, but coffeehouses were an upstart in New York (although already appearing in other cities). The next year Art D'Lugoff launched The Village Gate, a fancier establishment that would long feature folk and jazz performers, comics, musicals and much else. D'Lugoff had begun offering folk shows in 1955 at local theaters before having his own club, with Pete Seeger as the initial act. The legendary Gerde's Folk City would follow in 1960, commencing a decade full of clubs and coffeehouses.

There were also a growing number of record companies, allowing commercial outlets for the burgeoning folk scene.

GREENWICH VILLAGE

Greenwich Village is located on Manhattan Island in the heart of New York City. By the 1920s the increasing population of artists, actors, musicians, and writers, lured by the low rents, generally tolerant neighbors, and a European-style cultural ambience, had set the stage for a vibrant musical life that has lasted into the twenty-first century. In the 1920s nightclubs and cabarets began to emerge. In 1925 Paul Robeson opened at the Greenwich Village Theater with a show of all African-American songs, both religious and secular, a landmark musical evening that presaged his stellar musical career. Max Gordon opened the Village Vanguard in February 1934, and featured an eclectic mix of poetry and music. In late 1941, the Vanguard became the local home for a variety of folk music performers, then crowding into the Village, beginning with Josh White and Lead Belly, with Pete Seeger, Burl Ives, Richard Dyer-Bennet, and Woody Guthrie in the audience.

In late 1940 Seeger met Lee Hays and his roommate Millard Lampell, a budding writer, and the three soon moved into an industrial loft in the Village. Joined by Peter Hawes, Guthrie, Bess Lomax, sister of Alan, Sonny Terry and Brownie McGhee, and Agnes "Sis" Cunningham (along with her husband Gordon Friesen) they became the Almanac Singers, hosting Sunday afternoon musical rent parties as they developed a repertoire of traditional and topical songs. They performed and recorded extensively before disbanding in 1942, a pioneering assemblage of singer/songwriters, with Greenwich Village as their physical and spiritual home.

Pete Seeger and Lee Hays, along with Ronnie Gilbert and Fred Hellerman, formed the more structured Weavers in 1949 and opened at the Village Vanguard during Christmas week. After a slow start the crowds picked up, and the weeks stretched into six months, launching the Weavers on their exceptionally successful, but brief, career. As for the Vanguard, it remained a major jazz, folk, and comedy club. For those seeking a more rustic setting during the early 1940s, the Village Barn on West 8th St. featured square dancing, potato games, turtle races, and midnight waltzes. Art D'Lugoff had

begun staging folk concerts at the Circle-in-the Square Theatre in November 1955, and after a year switched to the Actor's
Playhouse, a prelude to opening the Village Gate in 1958. He
first booked Pete Seeger, followed by Earl Robinson, and soon
a host of jazz, folk, and comedy acts.

The Village experienced an upsurge of musical venues—coffee houses, clubs, and the like—in the late 1950s, accommodat-
ing the performers who flocked to the Village and the folk and
jazz audiences. Jac Holzman moved to Greenwich Village in
late 1951 and began hanging around Peter Carbone's Village
String Shop. He launched Elektra Records in 1952 out of his
store the Record Loft on West 10th St., specializing in folk and
Baroque records. Within a few years Elektra would become
one of the premier folk (and later pop) labels, located in the
Village until the move to Los Angeles in the 1960s. Elektra
was soon followed by Tradition Records, launched in 1956 by
Patrick Clancy and his brothers Tom and Liam, with the financial support of Diane Hamilton, and located on Christopher
Street. Tradition Records released the Clancy Brothers, Ed
McCurdy, Odetta, Robin Roberts, Ewan MacColl, and a host
of other tradition-based performers.

Washington Square, in the heart of the Village, on warm
Sunday afternoons was developing as a folk magnet, allowing
amateur (and even some professional) musicians the chance
to demonstrate their musical abilities, a tradition begun just
after World War II. Neighborhood musicians, such as Dave
Van Ronk, Mary Travers, John Sebastian, played in the
Square. One activist group of performers and fans, the Folksingers Guild, organized by Van Ronk and his friends in 1957,
held monthly concerts in local halls, often at midnight when
the space was available. Also in 1957 Israel G. "Izzy" Young
opened the Folklore Center on MacDougal Street, soon mecca
for folk singers and fans.

By 1959 the Village overflowed with coffeehouses, clubs, theaters, and a variety of other entertainment venues, but there
was little opportunity for folk singers until Izzy Young, who
had been producing his own concerts, with Peggy Seeger,
Oscar Brand, and the Rev. Gary Davis, opened the Fifth Peg in
January 1960. The Fifth Peg soon closed but quickly reopened

as Gerdes Folk City, which became the premier folk establishment, featuring, among others, Jean Ritchie, Cynthia Gooding, John Lee Hooker, Ramblin' Jack Elliott, as well as newcomers Bob Dylan, Judy Collins, John Phillips, José Feliciano, and Richie Havens. Other folk clubs included the Gaslight, Trudy Heller's Versailles, Fred Weintraub's Bitter End (previously the Cock 'n' Bull and later owned by Paul Colby), Rick Allmen's Café Bizarre, Manny Roth's Café Wha?, Feenjon's (featuring Turkish, Arabian, and Greek music and dancing), and assorted others. Friction between the Sunday folk singers in Washington Square and the local community resulted in a brief legal ban on instruments in 1961 that was revoked by the city following a mass demonstration in April.

The folk revival peaked in the mid-1960s, somewhat replaced by folk-rock, and in the Village newer and older clubs began booking rock and pop musicians, including Cafe Au Go-Go (soon the Gaslight Au Go-Go), which featured singer/songwriters as well as rock bands, and the Night Owl, with a more psychedelic orientation. The Village was attracting Linda Ronstadt, Joni Mitchell, Jackson Browne, Kris Kristofferson, Jimi Hendrix, and a host of other upcoming musical stars. Allan Pepper and Stanley Snadowsky opened the Bottom Line in the early 1970s, as the Village was losing much of its musical luster. The Vanguard and the Village Gate continued to feature top jazz musicians, however, while rock and folk performers had a variety of possibilities, although many of the clubs had already folded. Izzy Young continued to produce concerts until he closed the Folklore Center and permanently moved to Sweden in 1973.

A fledgling group of singer/songwriters, such as Suzanne Vega, Shawn Colvin, and John Gorka, were attracted to the SpeakEasy, opened in late 1981 (and closed in 1989) by Jack Hardy and Brian Rose. In early 1982 the first issue of *Fast Folk Musical Magazine* appeared, each issue an album featuring budding performers; in 1984 a yearly Fast Folk Revue began at the Bottom Line. *Fast Folk* ended in 1997. By century's end there were few clubs featuring folk music, with the exception of the Bottom Line, which closed in 2004. But the Village still served as a haven for many folk musicians.

Folkways Records, replacing Moe Asch's earlier Disc label in 1949, began issuing an escalating stream of the new 33 rpm albums, and among the more commercial companies Decca produced the Weavers and other folk favorites. In 1950 Jac Holzman, a college student, initiated Elektra Records, and after moving to New York City he opened a record store and began producing albums by Jean Ritchie, Cynthia Gooding, and Sonny Terry. By mid-decade it was going strong. The Clancy Brothers, Irish singers and actors, began Tradition Records in 1956, to record themselves as well as Jean Ritchie and Paul Clayton. Bill Grauer and Orrin Keepnews had launched Riverside Records as a jazz label in 1953, but when they hired Kenneth Goldstein as a producer in 1955 he began their Folklore Series, featuring Ed McCurdy, Clayton, Oscar Brand, Bob Gibson, and the British singers A. L. Lloyd and Ewan MacColl, whom he had previously included when he worked for Stinson Records. Maynard and Seymour Solomon had started Vanguard Records in 1950 as a classical label, but they also branched into folk music, beginning with blues man Brother John Sellers, and particularly the Weavers 1955 reunion concert at Carnegie Hall; this influential album appeared in 1957. Thus, by decade's end there were numerous folk labels—Folkways, Stinson, Riverside, Elektra, Vanguard, Tradition—supplying the mounting audience with a diversity of musicians and songs.

Folk music temporarily took a variety of interesting forms. In addition to the traditional Anglo-Saxon ballads and folk songs, as well as blues numbers and more recent compositions by Lead Belly and Guthrie, there was also a remarkable range of music available from throughout the world (Alan Lomax was far from alone in his interest in international music). The Weavers, with their commitment to world peace and understanding, had a broad repertoire, and they were joined by Cynthia Gooding, who issued an album of *Turkish and Spanish Folksongs* and another of *Mexican Folksongs*. Martha Schlamme had *German Folk*

Songs on the Folkways label, while Israeli numbers were performed by Hillel and Aviva, the Oranim Zabar, and Theo Bikel; Marais and Miranda were particularly popular singing songs from South Africa and various European countries. In recalling the Greenwich Village music scene, which was somewhat duplicated around the country, Dave Van Ronk has noted: "Someone would go off to Mexico or Greece and come back with a few new songs, or someone would stumble across an album of African cabaret music and learn a couple of tunes." In another twist, Ed McCurdy issued a series of racy albums, such as *Barroom Ballads*; *Blood, Booze 'n' Bones*; *Sin Songs*; and particularly four albums for Elektra labeled, *When Dalliance Was in Flower and Maidens Lost Their Heads*. These latter included double-entendre Elizabethan era songs, with very suggestive lyrics, that sold well. Will Holt had already recorded *Pills to Purge Melancholy*, drawn from Thomas D'Urfey's collection *Wit and Mirth: Or Pills to Purge Melancholy*, published in 1719–1720. Simultaneously, Oscar Brand began an extremely popular series of *Bawdy Songs and Backroom Ballads* on the Audio Fidelity label. Many of the songs he edited to tone down the lyrics, but they were still considered sexy and therefore became big sellers among college students into the 1960s. Generally, the international songs and bawdy compositions did not last much past the 1950s, but do give an indication of the fascinating scope of folk music at the time.

While folk music was thriving in New York City, home for most of the folk labels and performers, there were also revival stirrings elsewhere in the country. In Chicago, for example, there was a thriving folk music club at the University of Chicago, formed in 1953, as well as the University of Wisconsin, which brought Pete Seeger and others to campus. (Indeed, Seeger spent much of the decade performing at colleges and also children's summer camps, where the Left's folk legacy was deftly carried forward despite the harsh political climate.) Also, in Chicago, two vital institutions soon developed. Albert Grossman and Les Brown opened the Gate of Horn in 1956, a folk club that quickly featured Odetta, Big Bill Broonzy, and Theo Bikel. The Gate became the center of a vibrant folk scene. The following year musician Frank Hamilton and a group of local folk fans opened the Old Town School of Folk Music to teach music classes and sponsor concerts. The school grew rapidly (and is going strong 50 years later). The school not only focused on traditional American folk music, but also connected with the city's Greek, Polish, Serbian, and Croatian neighborhoods, demonstrating the universal nature of the music.

Los Angeles had no central neighborhood for folk music, such as Greenwich Village, but nourished various groups and locations. In 1957 Theo Bikel and Herb Cohen opened the Unicorn on Sunset Boulevard, a folk coffeehouse, and the following year opened Cosmo Alley, a folk nightclub. Spotting the possibilities, Ed Pearl, already active in UCLA's Folk Song Club, with weekly hootenannies (folk concerts), opened the Ash Grove in 1958, which remained the prime folk club for many years. San Francisco's folk scene included the hungry i, a club featuring folk music, jazz, and humor beginning in 1952. There were local folk groups, particularly the Gateway Singers. Across the bay in Berkeley, Barry Olivier had a local folk radio program and also staged folk concerts on and near the campus of the University of California. From these he launched the summer Berkeley Folk Festival in 1958, with Marais and Miranda, Jean Ritchie, and a few others. While not original—folk festivals were held at colleges in Pennsylvania in the 1930s, as well as at the Fort Valley State College in Georgia, Swarthmore College had hosted a folk festival since 1945, and Oberlin followed suit in 1957—the Berkeley festival soon became the country's largest on a college campus.

Folk festivals were held in other parts of the country as well, giving prizes and a chance for local performers to demonstrate their musical and dance skills. Indeed, grass-roots folk music was alive and well, as the numerous festivals readily demonstrated. The National Folk Festival had begun in 1934, and was going strong through the 1950s, mostly held in St. Louis until 1955, then Oklahoma City and Nashville, until moving to Washington, D.C. in 1960. The Oklahoma City festival, for example, included the usual wide range of musical and dance styles: Native American, British ballads, Spanish American folk songs, Morris and Square dancing, Ozark folk songs, Latvian music, and much more. The regional festivals were generally much more focused, for example the Carolina Folk Festival in Chapel Hill (starting in 1948), the Western Folklore Festival in Denver (beginning in 1941), the Arkansas Folk Festival in Fayetteville (starting in 1947), the Ozark Folk Festival in Eureka Springs (started in 1948), and the All-Florida Folk Festival in White Springs (launched in 1953).

Bascom Lamar Lunsford continued his Mountain Dance and Folk Festival in Asheville, now attracting hundreds of performers and thousands of spectators. Mainly featuring string bands, square dancing, and old ballads, Lunsford also included a group of Cherokee Indians. The Union Grove Fiddlers' convention in North Carolina sprang up in 1924, and was going strong through the 1950s and after. It had attempted to cling to its traditional string-band format, but caved into modern pressures, as noted in a 1957 article: "Rock 'n Roll has invaded the hallowed sanctums of the old time fiddlers convention! Yielding to the times and changing taste of the public, the convention officials divided the cash prizes into two divisions, one for performances of 'old time' music and the other for renditions aimed at more modern demands, including calypso and rock 'n roll." Now "Blue Suede Shoes" and "Hound Dog" competed with the traditional "Soldiers Joy" and "Black Mountain Rag." Northern musicians were also soon competing, including

Mike Seeger, Bob Yellin, and the Greenbriar Boys, a trend escalating through the 1960s.

Regional and college folk festivals had usually reached a limited audience and often contained traditional music and dance styles, although this was gradually changing. The advent of the Berkeley festival somewhat broke this mold, but it was the launching of the Newport Folk Festival in July 1959 that first included a variety of popular performers and garnered national publicity. Jazz musician and club owner George Wein had initiated a jazz festival in Newport, Rhode Island, a wealthy tourist spot, in 1954. Five years later he hit upon running a separate folk festival, and hired Albert Grossman from Chicago as the producer. The two days included a broad array of talent, including Odetta, Jean Ritchie, Pete Seeger, Martha Schlamme, Brownie McGhee and Sonny Terry, the New Lost City Ramblers, and the Kingston Trio. It was a great success, with Robert Shelton in *The New York Times* proclaiming it "perhaps the most ambitious attempt ever made at delineating a cross-section of the nation's folk music." The young Joan Baez was introduced by Bob Gibson, which would quickly launch her career as the folk queen. The festival grew the next year to three days and a rich mix of traditional, popular, black and white performers. Highlights from both festivals soon appeared on record. England had no comparable folk festival presence, although the Beaulieu Jazz Festival, launched in 1956 and influenced by the skiffle movement, would attract a large crowd and serve as a model.

THE KINGSTON TRIO

As the decade wound down there were increasing signs of a burgeoning folk music revival. Bob Shane, Dave Guard, and Nick Reynolds, as the Kingston Trio, seemed to appear from nowhere when they captured the public's imagination in mid-1958 with their recording of "Tom Dooley," which reached number one on the pop music charts just before Christmas. Influenced by the Weavers, who had regrouped a few years earlier but had not regained the immense popularity they had achieved at decade's beginning, the Kingston Trio again demonstrated that folk music, in popular packaging, had great commercial potential. Pete Seeger had always characterized himself as a singer of folk songs, and not a folk singer, to differentiate himself from traditional performers. Shane and Guard, had grown up in Hawaii, while Reynolds was from San Diego. They met in San Francisco in 1957, and quickly developed a slick style, picking up songs from a variety of sources. Their first album for Capitol, *The Kingston Trio*, appeared during the next summer, and included "Fast Freight" (from the Easy Riders), "Saro Jane" (from the Gateway Singers), "Sloop John B" (Weavers), "Hard, Ain't It Hard" (Guthrie), "Bay of Mexico" (Seeger), and "Tom Dooley."

By this time there were various folk groups searching for popularity—Gateway Singers, Easy Riders, Tarriers, Weavers—but none had the skill, appeal, and luck to hit the jackpot. "Tom Dooley" soon appeared as a single and caught fire. Tom Dooley (originally Dula), a Civil War veteran, was arrested in North Carolina in 1867 and convicted of the murder of Laura Foster; he was hanged the following year. Event ballads soon appeared, and Henry Whitter recorded a version with his partner G. B. Grayson in the 1920s. Frank Warner collected another version by Frank Proffitt in 1938, Alan Lomax published it in *Folk Song U.S.A.* in 1947, and Warner recorded it for Elektra in 1952. "Tom Dooley" was well known by the time the Trio included it in their first album, but its popularity was totally unexpected. The Kingston Trio appeared at both the Newport jazz and folk festivals in 1959, a singular achievement, and soon recorded numerous other albums and a broad array of songs. Their version of "M.T.A.," for example, caught on and became their second most requested number, although originally written in 1949 to support a Socialist candidate for mayor in Boston. They remained popular for many years, kicking off a folk revival that lasted into the midsixties. In their striped shirts and neat grooming they appeared a safe contrast to the greasy, sexy rock and rollers, who were not doing very well at the time, what with Elvis in the Army and other popular performers either dead or scattered. Moreover, the Trio didn't carry the taint of left-wing politics that had long plagued folk music. They shared the stage on the Roy Rogers and Dale Evans television show in early 1959 with Johnny Cash, Jimmy Dean, the Everly Brothers, and Roy Acuff. "It is hard to recall an instance when as wholesome a group of entertainers as the Kingston Trio has won as swift and widespread a popularity as they have," *Redbook* magazine intoned. The Trio's popularity rankled many folk performers and fans, however, who thought they were a corrupting influence, watering down the "pure" folk sounds, but others would testify that popular folk music led them to the more authentic kind. "Crew-cuts! Crew-cuts up the wazoo. And most of the music was so precious, so corny, you could lose your lunch," Dave Van Ronk has colorfully remembered. But the traditional performer Arthel "Doc" Watson later confessed: "I'll tell you who pointed our noses in the right direction, even the traditional performers. They got us interested in trying to put the good stuff out there—the Kingston Trio. They got me interested in it."

DECADE ENDS

Soon after Alan Lomax returned to the United States, despite a hectic schedule, he organized a major concert at Carnegie Hall in April 1959, making his mark on the developing Revival. Once again demonstrating his wide-ranging musical reach, the "Folksong '59" show included Arkansas singer Jimmy Driftwood, the gospel group Selah Jubilee Singers, blues performers Muddy Waters and Memphis

Slim, the Stony Mountain Boys playing bluegrass (a first at Carnegie Hall), Pete and Mike Seeger, the rock and roll group the Cadillacs, and Lomax himself doing prison work songs. It was certainly an eclectic concert. "The time has come for Americans not to be ashamed of what we go for, musically, from primitive ballads to rock 'n' roll songs," Lomax explained, he and generally received good reviews. Indeed, despite the obvious popularity of the Kingston Trio, other folk music styles were appearing or holding their own, although for a more limited audience. One example was the New Lost City Ramblers, who kicked off a revival of string-band music that has continued for many decades. John Cohen and Tom Paley, both skilled musicians, began performing together at Yale University in 1952. They began playing with Mike Seeger, brother of Pete, in mid-1958, and they soon recorded for Folkways Records. They attempted to duplicate the sounds of southern string-bands recorded in the 1920s and 1930, for example Gid Tanner and his Skillet Lickers, Charlie Poole and the North Carolina Ramblers, and Dr. Smith's Champion Horse Hair Pullers. Beginning in New York City, they appeared at the first Newport Folk Festival, and within a few years would launch an old-time music revival that included not only young newcomers, but also many of the original performers.

The New Lost City Ramblers were connected to a larger movement to recognize old-time and bluegrass music as part of the country's folk music legacy. For example, college student and future traditional performer Alice Gerrard was living in Washington, D.C. in 1957 with her husband Jeremy Foster, an old friend of Mike Seeger. On weekends they would "go up the country to the music parks, which were flourishing north of Baltimore at that time. There was Sunset Park, New River Ranch, Watermelon Park, and others," she has recalled. "Bill Monroe, Flatt and Scruggs, Jim and Jesse, the Stanley Brothers would play there." They were also listening to the Harry Smith *Anthology of American Folk Music* and visiting with old timers who were playing traditional banjo and fiddle tunes. "There was never a divide in my mind between the two [old-time and bluegrass music], but I was more immediately involved in bluegrass." This was another aspect of the developing revival that would definitely grow within a few years, particularly among young people in the North.

British folk musician and journalist John Hasted traveled to the United States in 1958 and visited with Woody Guthrie at the hospital in New Jersey. "Woody's affliction made talking difficult, singing equally so, and guitar-playing almost impossible," he recalled. "All we could do was to bring Woody news that People's Songs were alive and well, in Britain as well as the U.S.A." Hasted personified the transatlantic connection that would continue to flourish.

By decade's end folk music, however defined, had captured a new audience and numerous commercial outlets in the United States, and less so in Great Britain. "The music was acoustic and fresh, simple rhythms and gentle voices," Ellen Sander would recall, "a relief from the vinyl love masquerading as radio rock and roll. Audience would clap and stomp along and participate in the music they were experiencing." But this was only the beginning of a true folk music revival.

5

THE SIXTIES

GREAT BRITAIN

Folk music had not reached such popularity in the British Isles in the late 1950s that it was achieving in the United States, but there were stirrings of a movement that would soon escalate. It would also be a mix of traditional songs and styles along with newer interpretations and developments. Moreover, there was continuing musical cross-fertilization across the Atlantic.

"Folk-song in Britain is in an interesting condition," A. L. Lloyd explained in 1961. "Indeed, the condition is so far advanced that she is already in travail. Some say she's brought to bed of a monster, and others that she's about to lay a golden egg. The offspring will surely be a hybrid, but perhaps none the worse for that." He feared that the number of traditional singers was rapidly shrinking, just as professional musicians, folk clubs, and folk records were proliferating. He welcomed "that the present revival in folk-music shows some left-wing political colouring. In view of the history of the revival, matters could hardly be otherwise." He lamented the general academic refusal to study industrial folklore. Indeed, unlike Ireland, which had a national Folk-Lore Commission, and Scotland, with its School of Scottish Studies, England had no official folklore institution: "Mainly through lack of official encouragement and support, folk-song studies in England are in a low condition that falls far short of modern scientific standards shown elsewhere in Europe." The private EFDSS was perhaps the English substitute, with its music festivals, publications, and other programs.

Lloyd was encouraging the study and performance of workers and topical songs throughout Great Britain, while popular folk songs increased, but he was not totally disappointed. The arrival of an American submarine armed with Polaris nuclear missiles in Scotland in 1961 resulted in large demonstrations and a spate of antinuclear songs, such as "Ye'll No Sit Here" and "Ding Dong Dollar." The next year Folkways Records released the album *Ding Dong Dollar: Anti-Polaris and Scottish Republican Songs Recorded in Scotland*. The peace movement had been building in England as well, beginning in 1958 with a march to Aldermaston, the H-Bomb research center, from London. Numerous antiwar songs appeared, such as "The H-Bomb's Thunder" (to the tune "Miner's Lifeguard"), "Brother, Won't You Join In The Line?" (to the tune of "Buddy, Won't You Roll Down The Line"), and Ewan MacColl's "The Dove" (from "The Cuckoo"). The singing peace movement, along with the continuing interest in workers songs, would somewhat mark the British revival.

Topic Records, which had survived in the fifties, now faced increasing troubles because of competition and the shrinking of the Communist Party. Other labels produced folk records, such as Pye, which distributed Elektra's catalog, and Decca. Topic's release of the album *The Iron Muse: A Panorama of Industrial Folk Songs Arranged by A. L. Lloyd* in 1963, did have an important impact, however.

Recorded by Lloyd, Matt McGinn, Louis Killen, Ray Fisher, and Ann Briggs, the record introduced a younger audience to the country's industrial musical legacy. "In the wake of a great deal of abandonment of Communist party ideals within the folk scene, together with the mass recognition of the Beatles the same year, the album's critical regionalism and depleted political proselytising struck an appealing chord, firstly amongst the folk clubs and then among the general public," historian Michael Brocken has explained. While much of folk music had no political overtones, there was always room for a class-conscious element. Moreover, Topic would continue to turn out albums with a wide range of styles and performers, from across the world, through the century.

Increasing folk festivals and magazines would be another indication of the quickening revival. *Sing* was still going strong, but was joined by *Spin* in late 1961. The editor's modest notice that "'Spin' hopes to join with 'Sing,' 'Folk Bag,' and 'English Folk Song and Dance' in catering for a new public eager for songs to sing and information about songs and singers" appeared in the thin first issue. Within a few years, the slim magazine was appearing in a slick cover. "For the most part the songs and articles in *Spin* lean towards British traditional material and regular features have been Stan Hugill's shanty column, Leslie Haworth's ballad series, and now we are happy to have Blues authority Paul Oliver writing for us too," editor Beryl Davis proudly announced in 1966. *Folk Music* began publishing in late 1963, with Karl Dallas as an editor. He explained that *Sing* was no longer doing its job, so "as it seemed more and more likely that folk music might break through into the Hit Parade, the need for a literate folk magazine became acute." The first issue contained long articles by both MacColl and Lloyd, indicating its connection to the Communist Party. All of the magazines contained book and record ads, concert notices, and strong indications of the importance of American folk songs and performers, particularly Woody Guthrie, Pete Seeger, Jack Elliott, Bob Dylan, and Joan Baez. There was also *Folk Scene*, which included mostly printed songs, and the Scottish *Chapbook* by mid-decade. *Sing* continued to come out as well, in a larger format beginning in 1967, with songs, old and new, as well as album and record reviews.

Folk festivals also proliferated, seemingly offering something for everyone. The Aberdeen folk festival was launched in 1963, featuring Scottish performers as well as Tom Paxton, a leading American singer/songwriter. Festivals continued at the Cecil Sharp House in London, the sixth held in 1964, with The Spinners and Louis Killen. The following year, the Cambridge City Council initiated a folk festival that would grow over the coming decades. It included a mix of British and American performers, such as the Clancy Brothers, Shirley Collins, Peggy Seeger, Hedy West, Isla Cameron, and the Watersons. The next year Doc Watson, Cyril Tawney, Martin Carthy and Dave Swarbrick, and a few from the first year were presented, mixing British and American performers that would continue through the decade. Other festivals, such as one sponsored by the Manchester and District Peace Committee in 1966, featured pretty much only English performers, such as The McPeake family, Matt McGinn, and the Young Contemporaries; the Royal Albert Hall festival in 1968 had the Watersons and Al Steward. In any case, by decade's end there was a wide array of performers and styles available.

Simultaneously, the blues scene was expanding. "Brownie McGhee and Sonny Terry went to England in 1958 for the first of many visits," Paul Oliver explains, "and the same year Muddy Waters and Otis Span played in Europe. At first Waters's electric guitar was unacceptable to many listeners unaware of the changes that had taken place in Chicago blues." The American Folk Blues Festival, a group of traditional as well as electric/urban blues performers, toured Europe and England in 1964.

Sam "Lightnin'" Hopkins, Sleepy John Estes, Howlin' Wolf, Willie Dixon, and Sonny Boy Williams appeared at the Fairfield Hall in Croydon, further influencing a blues movement that had already taken off. The next year the British audience could see Big Mama Thornton, Buddy Guy, J. B. Lenoir, Roosevelt Sykes, and Mississippi Fred McDowell.

FOLK CLUBS AND THE CHANGING SCENE

By mid-decade the British folk scene was a combination of traditional and contemporary songs, American folk and blues performers, and so much more. "Until recently, the London folk-music scene consisted of recitals attracting specialized audiences," a *New York Times* piece noted in early 1961. "But today a typical Saturday night will find some 200 youngish people jammed into a room on Soho Square to hear the show of the Ballads and Blues Association. The folk singers they listen to include A. L. Lloyd, Peggy Seeger, Ewan MacColl, Robin Hall and Jimmie MacGregor, Steve Benbow's Folk Four and Nadia Cattouse, Shirley Collins, Jeannie Robertson and Isla Cameron." Other performers appeared at the Partisan Coffee-House in Soho and the Troubadour in Chelsea. One of the more controversial issues was the plan in some clubs to insist that performers only perform music from their own nationality background. "While folk music from the United States had previously been prevalent," historian Britta Sweers observes, "so strongly had British Irish folk music come to dominate the clubs that many musicians started to complain about their narrow-mindedness." Ewan MacColl initiated the policy at his Singers' Club, previously the Ballads and Blues Club, that performers could only perform songs in their native language and that they had grown up with. MacColl expressed his views in his magazine *Folk Music*, while those who preferred a more eclectic approach, particularly performing American folk and blues, controlled *Folk Scene*. Many opposed MacColl's seemingly rigid approach.

Two fresh directions were evident by mid-decade—the growth of blues-rock, inspired by American electric blues bands, in the hands of groups such as the Rolling Stones and John Mayall's Blues Breakers; and a new form of folk rock (or electric folk), focusing on traditional English and Irish songs and dance music, performed in a rock-band setting. While there might appear some overlap, these were divergent movements with transatlantic roots, influences, and connections. The blues had earlier come via performers and recordings, and was well known by the early 1960s. Alexis Korner and Cyril Davies had launched Blues Incorporated, first a band then a club, which began to attract young performers such as Brian Jones, Charlie Watts, Keith Richards, and Mick Jagger by 1962. One offshoot was the Rolling Stones (named for a Muddy Waters song), with Richards, Jagger, Jones, Dick Taylor, and Ian Stewart. "However, in the early 1960s there was a musical snobbishness around the musical mafia which looked down on the crude though sincere efforts of five white boys from the suburbs to play the blues," Bob Brunning, author of *Blues: The British Connection*, explains. This would soon become inconsequential as other white musicians picked up on the Chicago urban blues influence, just as the Beatles were also making their mark. Eric Clapton first joined the Roosters, then the Yardbirds in 1963, and so many others followed in his path. The Yardbirds even recorded with Sonny Boy Williamson in England. Through the remainder of the decade and on into the future the British blues groups would proliferate, with the Rolling Stones and Eric Clapton, among others, continuing into the twenty-first century.

ELECTRIC FOLK

Those who followed the path of electric folk were mostly steeped in traditional British folk music rather than American blues. "The various streams of folk-rock in Britain have been the product of this search within folk for themes, and of the dissatisfaction with the insularity of the traditionalist clubs felt by many younger musicians," Dave Laing explains. "The result is music for which rock provides the grammar and the various British traditional musics provide the vocabulary—either directly for the band Steeleye Span who adapt traditional songs *in toto,* or indirectly for Fairport Convention or Richard Thompson, who compose new songs using the elements of the tradition." Britta Sweers, in *Electric Folk: The Changing Face of English Traditional Music* (2005), has written the most comprehensive study of the rise and development of this musical style. She notes that the British folk revival began to be noticed in 1965 in *Melody Maker,* the popular music magazine, which initiated a "Focus on Folk" section. Folk rock now began to take shape, partly with "that unique duo Shirley Collins and Davy Graham," as *Melody Maker* mentioned (and somewhat parallel to the development in the United States).

After mid-decade various individuals initiated the multiple strands of the emerging electric folk scene: Shirley Collins and her sister Dolly, Martin Carthy and Dave Swarbrick, Davy Graham, Bert Jansch, John Renbourn, Sandy Denny, Richard Thompson, Ashley Hutchings, among many others. These performers formed the groups that would personify electric folk, although they differed significantly. Pentangle, for example, founded in 1966 by Renbourn and Jansch, incorporated old English ballads, American folk songs, classic jazz, and dance tunes of the renaissance in a unique style featuring exemplary guitar work. Their first two albums, released in 1968, *The Pentangle* and *Sweet Child,* attracted much enthusiasm. They toured extensively, appearing both at the Newport and Isle of Wight folk festivals in 1969. Fairport Convention, on the other hand, was formed in 1967 by Richard Thompson, Ashley Hutchings, and soon Sandy Denny, who introduced more traditional material. Their album *Liege & Lief* (1969), partly featuring electric versions of classic Child ballads, was a deft fusion of rock and folk, and included new members Dave Swarbrick, a virtuoso fiddler, and drummer Dave Mattacks. "In contrast with Pentangle," Sweers explains, "Fairport amplified all their acoustic instruments directly via electronic pickup." As for Steeleye Span, formed by Hutchings, formerly of Fairport Convention, in 1969, Sweers notes, "although the material was almost exclusively traditional, the instrumental sound, with its stronger emphasis on bass and later also drums, was much harder-edged." By decade's end electric folk was well established, part of the folk world, and would take various twists and turns for the rest of the century.

DECADE'S END

Lloyd published *Folk Song in England* (1967), the first broad overview of the topic. "I suppose what is newest in this book is the picture it offers of the continuity of folk song, from the 'classic' rural forms, through the urban industrial forms …, into that as yet vaguely chartered territory that lies between folklore proper and the realm of the commercial hit," he explains in the Preface, "an otherworld into which traditional songs in their resurrected form seem to integrate themselves quite happily, changed in function but still widely sung, listened to, and carried around in the head with love." Rather than expressing too much pessimism at folk music's commercial turn, he took heart that it was surviving, and perhaps even thriving. He would not include songs by the singer/songwriters, such as Bob Dylan and Donovan, as folk songs, however: "They may contain elements of alienation and protest, as certain folk songs do ..., but they still remain songs that firmly belong to the insubstantial world of the modern commercial hit and in no sense qualify to take their place alongside the home-made lyrics of the working people." Lloyd remained a traditionalist, while others were much more inclusive. Robin Denslow calls Donovan "a performer of some charm and limited talent," but his songs "Mellow Yellow" and "Sunshine Superman," were popular hits.

The British folk scene had something for everyone by decade's end, both highly influenced by the changing folk scene across the ocean, and also a singular product of native folk song and dance. Indeed, traditional music was still very much part of the revival. The Copper Family, for example, passed down the old songs through the generations, with Bob Copper performing into the 1960s. Their songs influenced Peter Bellamy and his trio Young Tradition. Shirley Collins also brought her family's songs into the folk scene, although in the 1970s her work with Ashley Hutchings briefly led her into the electric folk camp in the Albion Band. The Waterson family also performed vernacular songs in the 1960s, while the EFDSS continued to promote the old sounds.

THE UNITED STATES

During the early 1960s, it appeared as if all aspects of folk music's historical development—rural and electric blues, old-time string bands, topical/protest songs, traditional ballads and pop tunes, jug band music, domestic as well as foreign songs and musical styles, creative singer/songwriters, and even glitzy trios and quartets—came together to create a folk explosion. The folk revival contained extraordinary creative energy and serious political overtones, as well as fascinating aspects that would seemingly stretch the limits of commercial musical invention and exploitation. It was both more and less than the sum of its various musical parts. While this folk

JOAN BAEZ

Women had always been part of traditional folk music, but more often in the background than in the commercial spotlight. This would change with the folk revival, particularly due to the successful and long lasting career of Joan Baez. Born in Staten Island, New York, in 1941, she grew up in Northern California and moved with her family to the Boston area after high school. Briefly a student at Boston University, she preferred hanging around local folk clubs, and began performing at the Golden Vanity, Ballad Room, and particularly Club 47 in Cambridge. She appeared at the famed Gate of Horn in Chicago during the summer of 1959, and then the first Newport Folk Festival, as a guest of popular folksinger Bob Gibson. Her beautiful voice quickly led to her first album, *Joan Baez*, on Vanguard Records in 1960 and the start of a spectacular career. She first recorded "Silver Dagger," "Wildwood Flower," and "Mary Hamilton," which captured her interest in traditional English and American ballads and sparked their popularity.

Her amazing popularity was due not only to her lovely voice but also to her simple beauty, with her straight hair and penchant for performing shoeless, that challenged the ultrafeminine look of the 1950s. She toured widely and issued a steady stream of popular albums, including the two-record set *Joan Baez, Volume 2* (1961), *Joan Baez in Concert* (1962), *Joan Baez in Concert, Part 2* (1963), and many others. In 1963, she began introducing the newcomer Bob Dylan at her concerts, and their

explosion would last only a few years, its impact and legacy would resonate into the foreseeable future.

The developing youth market would be folk music's main audience. "The teenagers provide the momentum for most of the fads these days," Jay Milner explained in the *New York Herald Tribune* in early 1960, "and, as they did with rock and roll, teenagers are singing and playing folk music as well as listening to it." Alan Lomax added his interpretation for the readers of *House Beautiful*. While he recognized the popularity of the Kingston Trio, Harry Belafonte, and the Tarriers, he pointed out that "under the smooth relationship flourished for a brief time. They were known as the King and Queen of folk music, as detailed in David Hajdu's *Positively 4th Street: The Lives and Times of Joan Baez, Bob Dylan, Mimi Baez Fariña, and Richard Fariña* (2001). With her Quaker background, Baez also became involved in various protest movements, beginning with Civil Rights; in 1962 she performed at black colleges in the South, and appeared on 1963 March at Washington, along with the Reverend Martin Luther King. She supported the student Free Speech movement at the University of California, Berkeley in 1964, and then plunged into the growing antiwar movement as the war in Southeast Asia escalated. Her appearance at the 1969 Woodstock music festival capped her 1960s career.

She continued her performing and recording, as well as political activism, although with less popularity as the folk revival was pushed aside. Her one popular single, "The Night They Drove Old Dixie Down," reached number three on the Billboard chart in 1971. Vanguard released her First Ten Years album in 1970, and others followed from Vanguard and then other labels. She appeared at Phil Ochs's "War Is Over" Central Park concert in 1975, joined Dylan for his Rolling Thunder Review tour in 1975–1976, and also performed at the Live Aid concert in 1985. As her popularity waned in the United States, it lasted in the rest of the world into the 1990s. She continued her performing and activism into the next century, and would always remain as the female icon of the 1960s folk revival and protest movement.

bland surface of the popularized folk songs lies a bubbling stew of work songs, country blues, field hollers, hobo songs, prairie songs, spirituals, hoedowns, prison songs, and a few unknown ingredients." Lomax's views would become more popular within a few years. CBS-TV launched the one-hour *Folk Sound USA* show in June 1960, with Cisco Houston, Joan Baez, John Jacob Niles, Earl Scruggs and Lester Flatt, and Peter Yarrow. *Variety's* correspondent Harriett Van Horn complained that the mix of work songs, blues, and western ballads were "the kind of folk music I associate with far-out Bohemian types. I mean the kind who wear

leather thong sandals and entertain you after dinner (a cas-
serole of garlic bulbs and goat hearts, stewed in bad wine)
with their scratchy old recordings of blues songs by Leadbelly and Blind Willie Johnson." While perhaps tongue-
in-cheek, her views represented the lingering view of folk
music as something connected either with scruffy radicals
or southern rubes.

By the summer a quickening of interest was evident.
Both *Time* and *Newsweek* featured articles on folk music,
with the increasing popularity of Pete Seeger, Odetta, and
Theo Bikel. "The U.S. is smack in the middle of a folk-music
boom, and already the TV pitchmen have begun to take
advantage of it," *Time* seemed to be warning, somewhat
prematurely: "Pseudo folk groups such as the Kingston
Trio ... are riding high on the pop charts, and enthusiasm
for all folk singers—real or synthetic—has grown so rapidly that there are now 50 or so professional practitioners
making a handsome living where there were perhaps a half
dozen five years ago."

The second Newport Folk Festival in late June 1960 tried
to capture folk music's increasing eclectic nature. The three
dozen acts included Oscar Brand, the Clancy Brothers and
Tommy Makem, Pete Seeger, blues performers Robert Pete
Williams and John Lee Hooker, popular groups including
the Brothers Four and Bud and Travis, and Ewan MacColl.
"That was one of the greatest times, Newport," Hooker,
who played both acoustic and electric guitar, recalled. "The
'60s will never be forgotten, the memory will never die.
Great musicians like Brownie McGhee & Sonny Terry, and
Joan Baez and myself, and many, many more, blazed a trail
at Newport." George Wein, the festival's organizer, agreed:
"It was clear that the folk festival audience—mostly college age—found such meaning and honesty in the songs
themselves. Every night after festival's end, many of these
kids would take their sleeping bags to the beaches, setting
up little bonfires and trading folk songs well into the early

hours of the morning." Unfortunately, a riot the following week at the Newport Jazz Festival led to canceling the folk festival until 1963.

The quickening pace seemed ripe for a folk club in Greenwich Village. Izzy Young, whose Folkore Center was increasingly busy, tried to launch folk concerts at a local bar run by Mike Porco. The Fifth Peg opened in early 1960, with Ed McCurdy, the Clancy Brothers, the Tarriers, and Brownie McGhee and Sonny Terry. The crowds soon dwindled, however, and the Fifth Peg was replaced by Gerdes Folk City, which quickly became the premier folk establishment in the city. Perhaps it is best known as the place where Bob Dylan first gained fame. Born in 1941, Robert Zimmerman grew up in the mining town of Hibbing, Minnesota, and moved to Minneapolis in 1959 to enter the University of Minnesota. He loved all sorts of music, from Hank Williams and Jimmy Reed to the latest rock and roll performers, and had a series of garage bands in high school. He became a folk singer in Minneapolis, where he learned about southern blues and string bands, and particularly Woody Guthrie; he now became "Bob Dylan."

Dylan moved to New York in early 1961, where the action was to meet his new hero Woody Guthrie, still languishing in the state hospital in New Jersey. He quickly became a Village fixture, performing at various local cafés until his big break at Folk City on April 11. (Coincidentally, on April 9 there was a large protest in Washington Square Park because the city was trying to ban folk singing on Sunday afternoons, and Joan Baez was in town to join the protest. The next night she performed at Folk City, along with other protesters, including Dylan, which was the start of their friendship.) Dylan was the opening act for John Lee Hooker, who believed Dylan "had such good lyrics. He was a good writer. He learned stage presence. He might have learned a few tips from me but he never picked up my style, because he had his own thing. He was

BOB DYLAN

Robert Zimmerman, aka Bob Dylan, was born in Duluth, Minnesota, in 1941, although the family soon moved to the iron-mining town of Hibbing, where he grew up. He briefly attended the University of Minnesota, then moved to New York City at the beginning of 1961 in order to meet Woody Guthrie and become involved in the developing folk music scene in Greenwich Village. He visited Guthrie in the hospital in New Jersey and quickly came under the influence of Dave Van Ronk and other Village folk singers. He began hanging around Izzy Young's Folklore Center and playing at various local coffeehouses until getting his big break at Folk City, with a glowing review by Robert Shelton in The *New York Times* in late 1962.

Dylan recorded his first album for Columbia Records the next year, *Bob Dylan*, and began publishing in *Broadside* magazine, starting with "Blowin' in the Wind." His next album, *The Freewheelin' Bob Dylan* (1963) included some of his most creative topical songs, including "Don't Think Twice, It's All Right," "A Hard Rain's A-Gonna Fall," and "Blowin' in the Wind," launching him on a spectacular career that would continue into the next century. Drawing upon his seemingly encyclopedic knowledge of music history, his songs often borrowed from traditional folk and gospel tunes, producing a creative product that was highly influential.

The album *The Times They Are A-Changin'* (1963) included more of his topical output, with the title track, "Lonesome Death of Hattie Carroll," and "Only a Pawn in Their Game." While Dylan did not have hit singles with his songs, they were covered by Peter, Paul and Mary, who did, as well as numerous others. But Dylan was extremely popular, appearing at the Newport Folk Festivals and various civil rights events. But by 1965 he began to write more personal, introspective songs, such as "My Back Pages," "Chimes of Freedom," and "It Ain't Me Babe," which appeared on his album *Another Side of Bob Dylan* in 1964. He was now moving away from acoustic to electric instruments, with both appearing on his path breaking album *Bringing It All Back Home* (1965), with "Gates of Eden," "Tambourine Man," and "It's All Over Now, Baby Blue." The album and his appearance at the controversial Newport Folk Festival in 1965 marked his musical break with not only acoustic instruments, but also political songs, which generated some criticism. *Highway 61 Revisited* (1965) was his first all electric album, with the influential "Like a Rolling Stone." Now mostly using rock arrangements, he recorded *Blonde On Blonde* (1966), but he soon disappeared from public for a couple of years, seemingly recovering from a motorcycle accident.

By the late 1960s Dylan had settled into frequently changing his style, beginning with the mellow *John Wesley Harding* (1968), the country album *Nashville Skyline* (1969), the odd *Self Portrait* (1970), and numerous others through the 1970s, ending the decade with the born-again Christian songs of *Slow Train Coming* (1979), although this phase of his life was brief. For the rest of the century he maintained a hectic recording and concert life, with both old and new songs continuing to appear. There seemed to be no end to an interest in his life and songs, with numerous books and magazines devoted to inspecting every facet of his life, particularly in the United States and Great Britain, but also throughout Europe and Japan. He appeared to hit another creative high at century's end, with *Time Out of Mind* winning three Grammy awards in 1998, including Album of the Year. Dylan published *Chronicles* (2004), the first volume of his autobiography that achieved critical and popular acclaim. His early years have been well captured in the famed director Martin Scorsese's lengthy documentary film *Bob Dylan—No Direction Home* (2005).

Dylan's popularity and influence have been immense, both as a folk and rock singer/songwriter, although he continued to be most closely associated with the role of folk music in fueling and capturing the social upheavals of the 1960s.

strictly a folk singer." Dylan initially performed Guthrie and older songs, but soon included more of his own compositions, usually based on traditional tunes. Following his return to Folk City in late September, *New York Times* music reviewer Robert Shelton gave him a glowing sendoff: "Although only twenty years old, Bob Dylan is one of the most distinctive stylists to play in a Manhattan cabaret in months." Dylan was quickly signed to Columbia Records by legendary record executive John Hammond. While his first album, *Bob Dylan*, released in March 1962, filled with traditional songs such as "House of the Rising Sun" and "Freight Train Blues," had small sales, he was on his way.

Meanwhile, Joan Baez's career was flourishing, marking the coming folk explosion. She continued to record increasingly popular albums for Vanguard—her second album, *Joan Baez, Volume 2* (1961), remained on the *Billboard* pop charts for more than two years—performed around the country, and appeared on the cover of *Time* in late 1962. Earlier in the year the weekly news magazine had noted that "all over the U.S. people of all descriptions—young and middle-aged, students, doctors, lawyers, farmers, cops—are plucking guitars and moaning folk songs, happily discovering that they can amuse both themselves and their friends." Along with the November Baez cover photo, the Time reporter explained that folk performers could be divided into three categories: the Popularizers (Kingston Trio, Limeliters), the "Semipures, the Adapters, the Interpreters" (Baez, Guthrie, Seeger, Dylan), and the "Pures, the Authentics, the Real Articles" (Jean Ritchie, Frank Proffitt). There were an increasing number of performers in the first two categories, while the third would soon gain in importance and popularity. Baez, for example, was joined by a number of exciting female performers, including Judy Collins, who was soon recording for Elektra, Carolyn Hester, and Buffy Sainte Marie.

There were also a growing number of duos, trios, quartets, and even larger groups such as the New Christy

Minstrels. Many began as college students. The Brothers Four had formed in 1958 and signed with Columbia Records the next year; the Chad Mitchell Trio also formed in 1958; the Journeymen's first album appeared in 1961 on Capitol; the Rooftop Singers formed in 1962. This sampling of groups joined the Kingston Trio, the Limeliters, and even the Weavers, who were still recording and performing. Albert Grossman easily perceived the growing market for pop folk groups and launched his own search for a unique trio. In 1961 he created Peter, Paul and Mary. Peter Yarrow and Mary Travers were already established performers, while Noel Paul Stuckey was a singer and standup comic in Greenwich Village. Their first album for Warner Bros. appeared in March 1962 and stayed on the charts for an amazing 185 weeks. Their recording of "If I Had a Hammer" (originally "The Hammer Song," a peace song written by Lee Hays and Pete Seeger) sold quickly as a single, as did "Puff (The Magic Dragon)." They would soon popularize songs by Grossman's other major performer, Bob Dylan, starting with "Blowin' in the Wind."

TRADITIONAL FOLK

The growing popularity of the commercial folk performers, with their increasing publicity, was troubling to some, who preferred the seemingly authentic sounds of traditional blues and old-time musicians. Two undergraduates at the University of Minnesota, Jon Pankake and Paul Nelson, decided to promote their own version of "real" folk music with the launching of a small magazine, the *Little Sandy Review*, in early 1960. The editors mostly reviewed new albums, preferring those that reissued earlier blues and hillbilly recordings, and particularly Alan Lomax's Southern Folk Heritage Series for Atlantic Records. The *Little Sandy Review* had limited circulation but, surprisingly, growing influence, and the editors were far from alone in preferring the traditional performers. In 1961 student members of the Folklore Society at the University of Chicago launched a midwinter folk festival, featuring mostly older musicians. The previous year the New Lost City Ramblers had appeared on campus, part of their college tour, which sparked an interest in a festival. The first University of Chicago Folk Festival featured a large, racially mixed lineup, including Horton Barker, Frank Proffitt, Elizabeth Cotten, Roscoe Holcomb, Frank Warner, Willie Dixon, and Memphis Slim, along with the New Lost City Ramblers. Robert Shelton in *The New York Times* praised the festival: "In a period when the popularization of folk music had led to many specious species of dilution and hybridization, the bulk of the music at the festival was as pure and refreshing as a swig of spring water. The key words were tap-roots, tradition, authenticity, and non-commercial." The second festival featured Clarence "Tom" Ashley, Doc Watson, Big Joe Williams, the Reverend Gary Davis, Jean Ritchie, and the Staples Singers, the sort of roots lineup that would become increasingly popular.

The festival quickly sparked the founding of the Campus Folksong Club at the University of Illinois, under the direction of Archie Green, a university librarian and pioneer of research in hillbilly music. The club kicked off with a visit by the ubiquitous New Lost City Ramblers and a newsletter, *Autoharp*, which lasted until 1968. "If traditional folksong is to be heard on campus, other than via recording and tape, it must be heard by importing true folk singers, or by imparting to collegiate singers of folksongs some respect for traditional material and styles," Green explained. A steady stream of performers appeared on campus, including Sonny Terry and Brownie McGhee, Jimmy Driftwood, and the blues singer Curtis Jones. A similar Folk Song Club was launched at nearby Indiana University—Bloomington in 1962, which shared performers with the Illinois campus.

The preference for traditional music caught on in New York City, where Izzy Young, John Cohen, and performer/folklorist Ralph Rinzler formed the Friends of Old Time Music in late 1960. Their first concert in February 1961 included Roscoe Holcomb, Jean Ritchie, the Greenbriar Boys, a northern bluegrass group with Rinzler, and the New Lost City Ramblers. Future programs featured Clarence Ashley and Doc Watson, Bill Monroe, Bessie Jones, Gus Cannon, and Furry Lewis, all traditional musicians. Rinzler had recently discovered Ashley, who had first recorded in the 1920s, and the younger guitar wizard Watson, and after New York he brought them to the Chicago Folk Festival and then to the Ash Grove club in Los Angeles. Ed Pearl, Ash Grove's owner, had been booking more popular acts, but with Ashley and Watson, as well as the New Lost City Ramblers and blues performer Lightnin' Hopkins, he now focused on "what I felt was the real stuff—and have it slowly replace the more sophisticated stuff," as he later explained. Barry Olivier somewhat followed suit in 1961 with the Berkeley Folk Festival, which included Frank Warner, Jean Ritchie, and the Texas bluesman Mance Lipscomb, only recently discovered by Chris Strachwitz. Indeed, Strachwitz launched his own label, Arhoolie, in 1960 in order to issue Hopkins, Mance Lipscomb, and other roots musicians. The *Little Sandy Review* editors remarked that "when Sam Charters wrote his book, *The Country Blues* (1959), it was generally conceded that the era of genuine traditional blues recording was over. Such has not turned out to be the case—the well that looked very dry in 1959 is a veritable geyser in 1961."

While blues and hillbilly musicians who had never recorded, such as Lipscomb and Doc Watson, became popular at festivals and on records, there was a continuing search for older musicians who had ceased recording in the 1930s but could still be alive. Indeed, researcher Tom Hoskins unearthed Mississippi John Hurt in his hometown in 1963.

Sam Charters had found Walter "Furry" Lewis in Memphis in 1959, and four years later Booker "Bukka" White was also discovered living in Memphis; in 1964, Son House was discovered in Rochester, New York, and Skip James in Mississippi. "It was incredible, because we knew these guys from hearing them on old 78s, but it had never occurred to us that they would still be alive and playing, and now they were turning up all over the place," Dave Van Ronk recalled. "It got to be like the Old Blues Singer of the Month Club." The southern bluesmen now found themselves appearing at folk festivals and in recording studios for the first time in decades, along with older white musicians such as Dock Boggs, Roscoe Holcomb, Clarence Ashley, and Buell Kazee. The traditional musicians had an important influence on the folk revival, connecting past with present in personal terms.

TOPICAL SONGS

Topical/political songs had long been considered part of the country's folk heritage, stretching back to labor songs of the nineteenth century, through the songs of Joe Hill and the Industrial Workers of the World (IWW), and particularly during the 1930s with the rise of organized labor and the Communist Party. Woody Guthrie was only one of a number of topical songwriters, although certainly the most creative and influential. His influence would echo down through the decades, most importantly through the compositions of Bob Dylan, although he was far from the only young performer in the 1960s who took inspiration from the Oklahoma bard who, increasingly incapacitated, languished in a hospital until his death in 1967. Pete Seeger continued a prolific career not only as a performer, but also a songwriter.

Sis Cunningham had been a member of the Almanac Singers in the early 1940s, along with Seeger, Guthrie, and Bess Hawes, and by the 1950s she and her husband,

Gordon Friesen, were living in a housing project in New York City. Having been prompted by Seeger and Malvina Reynolds, another prolific topical songwriter, Cunningham and Friesen launched *Broadside*, a magazine subtitled "A Handful of Songs About Our Times," in February 1962. The quarterly *Sing Out!* published few contemporary songs, and it was becoming evident that there was a proliferation of songwriters and a market for their songs. "*BROADSIDE*'s aim is not so much to select and decide as to circulate as many songs as possible and get them out as quickly as possible," the editors declared. "*BROADSIDE* may never publish a song that could be called a 'folk song.' But let us remember that many of our best folk songs were topical songs at their inception." The first issue continued Reynolds's "Come Clean Blues" and Dylan's "Talkin' John Birch Society Blues," his first published song. Young songwriters, including Dylan, Tom Paxon, Phil Ochs, Len Chandler, and Peter LaFarge, would meet monthly in Sis and Gordon's cramped apartment and record their new songs, which would be transcribed and soon appear in the magazine. Budding artists from around the country began sending their tapes and song sheets to the magazine. In addition to songs, Broadside also published articles, letters, and numerous illustrations capturing the rapidly changing political climate of the 1960s. Dylan's "I Will Not Go Down Under the Ground," an antibomb shelter song, appeared in the third issue, and "Blowin' in the Wind" in the sixth. As Dylan's fame grew, he would leave the *Broadside* crowd, but through the decade the magazine continued to publish a wide array of topical songs (it did not fold until the 1980s). Moreover, in conjunction with Folkways Records, a number of albums were issued on the Broadside label featuring the music played at their apartment.

In the past, topical songs were often linked to the labor movement, but now the civil rights movement served as the inspiration for organizing songs, both old and new. Guy

AGNES "SIS" CUNNINGHAM
AND BROADSIDE MAGAZINE

Agnes "Sis" Cunningham was born in Watonga, Oklahoma, in 1909, the daughter of poor, but politically committed, farmers. She graduated from college and taught music for three years before her stay at Commonwealth College, Mena, Arkansas, in the early 1930s, where she performed and published *Six Labor Songs*. She next became an organizer for the Southern Tenant Farmers' Union and worked briefly as a music instructor at the Southern Summer School for Women Workers near Asheville, North Carolina, before returning to Oklahoma in 1939. There she helped organize the Red Dust Players, a traveling troupe that entertained and sought to mobilize the state's poor with radical songs and skits.

Sis met Gordon Friesen in early 1941 and they were soon married. The local attack on political radicals forced their move to New York City in November, where they quickly connected with the Almanac Singers and moved into Almanac House, along with Pete Seeger, Lee Hays, Bess Hawes, and Woody Guthrie; they were particularly close to Woody. Sis played with the group and appeared on their record *"Dear Mr. President."* She continued to perform through the 1940s, while raising two daughters, but was sidetracked by poverty and illness throughout the 1950s, while Gordon was blacklisted as a journalist.

In 1962 Sis and Gordon launched *Broadside*, a topical song magazine, which quickly published Bob Dylan, Tom Paxton, Phil Ochs, Malvina Reynolds, Frederick Douglas Kirpatrick, Eric Andersen, Janis Ian, and so many others. They also issued a number of Broadside albums, in conjunction with Folkways Records, and continued to publish *Broadside* until 1988, although it lost much of its market and influence after the 1960s.

Sis Cunningham was involved as a performer, songwriter, and promoter/publisher of folk music and topical folk songs beginning in the early 1930s. She was a seminal figure in promoting women's music, and her achievements (along with her husband Gordon) have been crucial in stimulating and promoting singer/songwriters for countless decades. She died on

June 27, 2004. *The Best of Broadside 1962–1988: Anthems of the American Underground from the Pages of Broadside Magazine*, a survey of recorded songs that appeared in the magazine, was issued by Smithsonian Folkways Recordings in 2000. The five CDs, with 89 songs, along with detailed liner notes, received two Grammy nominations, and serves as a monument to Sis and Gordon's vital role in promoting topical songs. Their book, *Red Dust and Broadsides: A Joint Autobiography*, was published in 1999, a wonderful story about their lives and hardships.

Carawan, a music director at the Highlander Folk School in Tennessee, originally formed in the 1930s to train labor organizers but recently a center of the civil rights movement, was instrumental in using music to promote the cause. He not only made a number of field recordings of the civil rights movement in various southern cities, most issued on Folkways Records, but he also introduced "We Shall Overcome" by 1960, which quickly became the civil rights anthem. Freedom songs soon proliferated, bringing a sense of solidarity and strength to those, mostly blacks and some whites, who were increasingly beaten and jailed as the southern protest movement gathered strength. The Student Non-Violent Coordinating Committee (SNCC), formed in 1960, and the older Congress of Racial Equality (CORE), along with Martin Luther King's newer Southern Christian Leadership Conference (SCLC), always used songs in their marches and demonstrations. The Freedom Singers, a quartet of SNCC workers, toured the country in 1963, raising money for the cause, and appeared at the Newport Folk Festival.

Broadside and *Sing Out!* were now filled with civil rights songs. Some, such as Dylan's "The Lonesome Death of Hattie Carroll" and "Ballad of Hollis Brown," were creative and thoughtful, but most, such as "We Shall Not Be Moved" and "Keep Your Eyes on the Prize," and of course

"We Shall Overcome," were designed as mass organizing tools, many derived from familiar gospel tunes. Bob Dylan, Odetta, Josh White, Joan Baez, and Peter, Paul and Mary performed during a morning premarch concert on the day of the historic March on Washington in August 1963. Later in the day Dylan, the Freedom Singers, Peter, Paul and Mary, the opera star Marian Anderson, and gospel diva Mahalia Jackson sang to the gathered throngs. Robert Sherman in the *Saturday Review* welcomed the appearance of professional musicians, but cautioned, "It is, of course, on the Southern battlefields of the war against discrimination, that these freedom songs have served, and are serving with the greatest effectiveness."

Popular black performers, with few exceptions—Harry Belafonte, Nina Simone, who performed "Mississippi Goddam"—were not directly involved in civil rights actions. (Soul/rhythm and blues musicians, such as Ray Charles and James Brown, represented black consciousness in their music, but they avoided overt civil rights concerts and events. Berry Gordy, owner of Motown, issued civil rights records, but was slow in urging his acts to get too involved.)

The Mississippi Freedom Summer project in 1964, designed to promote voter registration and freedom schools, included the Summer Caravan of Music, with Phil Ochs, Pete Seeger, Judy Collins, and Peter LaFarge giving concerts. Civil rights workshops in the South featured civil rights songs. For instance, in early 1965 a musical workshop in Mississippi included the Georgia Sea Island Singers, the Moving Star Hall Singers, Doc Reese, and Alan Lomax; all except Lomax were African American, representing the grass-roots nature of the music. Soon after, the first Northern District Mississippi Folk Festival was held, with only local musicians. At year's end another festival was held in Greenwood, in the heart of the Delta, with religious singing dominating. Freedom songs were also popular in the North, where a Freedom Folk Festival was held in Cambridge, Massachusetts, to raise money for CORE. The 40 performers included Tom Paxton, Pete LaFarge, Eric Andersen, and Ronnie Gilbert.

The civil rights movement led directly into campus organizing and demonstrations, beginning with the founding of Students for Democratic Society (SDS) in 1960 and the University of California, Berkeley Free Speech Movement (FSM) in 1964. Joan Baez quickly appeared at Berkeley to lead the students in singing "The Times They Are A-Changin'" and "We Shall Overcome" (the FSM leaders had just returned from civil rights work in Mississippi). Folk music would remain a feature of campus organizing, although college students were becoming attracted to folk rock, and rock and roll more broadly.

As fighting was escalating in Southeast Asia, with the United States committing a half-million troops by decade's end, folk music served as a rallying cry for the mounting peace movement. A "Sing-In For Peace" concert at Carnegie Hall in mid-1965 featured 60 performers, including Peter, Paul and Mary, Baez, and the Freedom Singers, and attracted 5,000 people. Peace songs served to focus the swelling crowds at the antiwar rallys. *Broadside* and somewhat *Sing Out!* continued to publish peace songs, old and new.

HOOTENANNY

"Hootenanny" is simply defined as "a meeting of folk singers, especially for public entertainment," but in the 1960s its meaning became much more expansive. Indeed, virtually everything connected with folk music became part of the hootenanny phenomenon. ABC-TV launched the *Hootenanny* show in early 1963, a half-hour on Saturday nights hosted by Jack Linkletter, the son of television personality Art Linkletter. The show was quite popular, and would stretch to one hour in the fall, until its cancellation for the network's fall 1964 lineup. Each week would find a group of musicians at a college campus, with the student audience as part of the program. The first program featured Bob Gibson, the Limeliters, Bud and Travis, and Bonnie Dobson at the University of Michigan, representing the sort of variety that would carry through the show's history.

But *Hootenanny* also had serious problems. Program heads refused to allow Pete Seeger or the Weavers to appear, claiming their lack of popularity, although it was clear that their past leftwing politics was the real issue. Immediately a boycott committee formed, and some of the most popular performers, such as Baez, Dylan, Peter, Paul and Mary, refused to appear. Judy Collins initially supported the boycott, but later did appear, as did the New Lost City Ramblers, which included Pete's brother Mike. *Hootenanny* would later be considered a flop, with a short life, and with "artistic direction to be slick and commercial," as Judy Collins would later complain, but at the time it was one of ABCs most popular shows and lasted through the peak of the folk revival. Moreover, there were no other prime time folk shows, although folk performers occasionally appeared on other programs. (CBS considered one titled *Folk Festival*, which might include Seeger, Baez, and Peter, Paul and Mary, but it was never produced.) For example, Dylan was scheduled for the Ed Sullivan Show in May 1963, but when the CBS-TV censors refused to allow him to sing "Talkin' John Birch Society Blues", he cancelled. And no network show would have any of the traditional performers, some of whom appeared on Pete Seeger's *Rainbow Quest* program, which had only limited distribution on educational television.

Hootenanny became a catchall term designed to promote folk music and sell products. In addition to the scores of Hootenanny compilation albums, featuring a wide array of folk performers, there was also *Jazz Swing Hootenanny*, *Hootenanny for Orchestra*, the children's albums *Kiddie Hootenanny* and *A Rootin' Tootin' Hootenanny*, *Surfin' Hootenanny with Tom and Jerry*, *Big Band Hootenanny*,

Gene Chandler's *Soul Hootenanny*, and *Soul Meeting Saturday Night Hootenanny Style* (with blues performers Jimmy Reed, John Lee Hooker, and Memphis Slim on the Vee-Jay label). Hollywood had a difficult time with folk music, with only one feature film, *Hootenanny Hoot*, with Johnny Cash, Judy Henske, Sheb Wooley, the Gateway Trio, and the Brothers Four, that also had a spin-off album. The exhibitor's promotional guide suggested that theaters could promote hootenannies in their lobbies or stage "Hootenanny Hoot" dance contests. There was a short-lived Bally Hootenanny pinball machine, Hootenanny Halloween costumes, and the Fuller Brush Company had a Hootenanny bath power mitt as well as Hootenanny hand lotion. Paperback songbooks poured off the presses, including *Hootenanny Tonight*, and there was even the novel *Hootenanny Nurse*. ("He brought a new song to her heart.") A Batman comic featured a story with "The Hootenanny Hotshots." There was even a package of "Hootenanny ABC-TV Paper Dolls," a Hootenanny bath towel, and so much else.

The time now seemed ripe for a slick folk music magazine, since *Sing Out!* still retained its small format and quarterly schedule, while *Broadside* (there was also a Boston *Broadside* and smaller *Broadsides* published in other cities), and the *Little Sandy Review* obviously had limited circulation and appeal. Robert Shelton of *The New York Times* launched *Hootenanny* magazine in December 1963, with songs, cartoons, features, and much more, a slick affair geared for the general market. Shelton defined folk very broadly, including traditional and modern, blues, bluegrass, flamenco, and work songs. But *Hootenanny* crashed after four issues, with the last featuring Shelton's piece "The Kingston Trio vs. Beatlemania." The rival *Folk Music* lasted for only two issues, a single issue of *Hootenanny Songs and Stars* appeared in 1964, while *ABC-TV Hootenanny Show Magazine*,

although with no formal connection to the show, survived for three issues. Local folk magazines popped up
in cities and small towns, as well as college campuses,
featuring songs, local news, reviews, and other bits of
information to connect the local scene to the broader
movement. There were few books to explain what was
happening, although Josh Dunson's *Freedom in the Air*
analyzed the topical song movement in 1965. Performer
Oscar Brand published the helpful *The Ballad Mongers:
Rise of the Modern Folk Song* in 1962, but it was not
until 1967 that David DeTurke and A. Poulin compiled
The American Folk Scene (1967), a handy anthology covering various aspects of the revival; the next year, photographer Dave Gahr and Robert Shelton published *The
Face of Folk Music* (1968), a wonderful compilation of
photos and text.

Hootenanny items and magazines came and went
within less than two years, as the revival quickly peaked
and partially collapsed. New Jersey's Palisades Amuse-
ment Park had a Miss Hootenanny Contest in 1963. Seven
thousand college students heard 36 folk groups competing for a Mercury Records contract during their spring
break at Daytona Beach. Perhaps 50 radio stations had
hootenanny radio shows. Men's magazines, in particular,
included articles on folk music, although all sorts of magazines had an interest in covering and interpreting what
seemed to be happening. Every city and college town had
a folk club, some quite posh, others in the dank basement
of a church. Guitar sales were skyrocketing, while banjos,
fiddles, and other assorted folk instruments had found a
healthy market. "Whether one sings, listens, ponders or
just beats time," music historian Arnold Shaw explained
in late 1964, "the folk frenzy is a matter for rejoicing,
reflecting as it does an affirmative change in temper of the
college generation, a still-to-be assessed turn from cool
spectatorism to active involvement."

FESTIVALS

The 1963 Newport Folk Festival, the first since 1960, had a stellar lineup representing all aspects of the unfolding folk scene. Peter, Paul and Mary, Dylan, Baez, Collins, and Seeger fulfilled the dreams of those who preferred the current stars. Bluegrass was represented by Bill Monroe and Jim and Jesse; traditional performers included Doc Watson, Clarence Ashley, John Lee Hooker, and Mississippi John Hurt; topical performers included the Freedom Singers and Tom Paxton; and there were assorted urban singers, such as Dave Van Ronk and Jackie Washington. The iconic final evening had Peter, Paul and Mary, Dylan, Baez, Seeger, Theo Bikel, and the Freedom Singers leading the crowd in "We Shall Overcome." There were now numerous other festivals, including the Jimmy Driftwood Arkansas Folk Festival, the Brandeis University festival, the Philadelphia Folk Festival, as well as the older ones at Berkeley and the University of Chicago, both of which preferred traditional to topical performers. Seemingly there was live music for everyone throughout the country, in addition to the countless concerts and hoots. Ed Pearl launched the UCLA festival in 1963 with Ashley, Roscoe Holcomb, Bill Monroe, the New Lost City Ramblers, and Pete Seeger, reflecting Pearl's growing interest in traditional music. Pearl was also involved with the first Monterey festival, which included a greater variety of styles, included not only Peter, Paul and Mary and Dylan, as well as Mance Lipscomb and Bill Monroe, but it drew a small crowd.

The 1964 Newport festival represented perhaps the height of the revival, stretching to four days and three nights. The usual cast of performers was joined by a freedom songs workshop, and evening concerts with Hawaiian songs, "Yank" Rachell, Elizabeth Cotten, Dylan, the Chad Mitchell Trio, Baez, Phil Ochs, and so many others. Many of the traditional musicians had been brought together by Ralph Rinzler, while Alan Lomax produced the opening night's "A Concert of Traditional Music." Some were disturbed that Dylan, appearing three times, introduced his more introspective songs, "It Ain't Me Babe," "Tambourine Man," and "All I Really Want to Do," indicating his turn away from topical songs that disturbed many in the audience. The next month's release of *Another Side of Bob Dylan* included "Motorpsycho Nightmare," and "My Back Pages," further evidence of his new approach.

Dylan's turn toward electric instruments and personal/disturbing lyrics became even clearer at the 1965 Newport festival. What began as a most promising event, with a very eclectic lineup, would also prove to be extremely controversial. There was an outstanding variety of performers, ranging from Memphis Slim, Lightnin' Hopkins, Son House, and Mance Lipsomb, to Richard and Mimi Fariña, English singer/songwriter Donovan, and old-time fiddler Eck Robertson, to Spokes Masiyane, a tin whistle player from South Africa. The Paul Butterfield Blues Band, a racially mixed group featuring Michael Bloomfield on guitar, performed during an afternoon blues workshop as well as during the Sunday night finale. The latter caused some controversy, since electric instruments were not usual and the sound system was not set up to cover their range and volume. But the greatest disturbance occurred when Dylan appeared on stage with an electric guitar and some members from the Butterfield band. They only played three songs, "Maggie's Farm," "Like a Rolling Stone," and "It Takes a Train to Cry," which is all they had quickly rehearsed earlier that day, then Dylan left the stage. Whether there was more booing than cheering is still controversial, although obviously some in the audience were offended by the inadequate sound system and loud playing, while others were disappointed that Dylan had left so quickly. Dylan was persuaded to return to the stage with an acoustic guitar, and he ended with "It's All Over Now, Baby Blue" and "Mr. Tambourine Man," to wild applause. "The repercussions were huge," festival promoter George Wein believed; "no longer was there the semblance of a pure folk community that resisted corruption by outside forces. Instead, distinctions were blurred. The young idealistic folk fans, who had valiantly resisted the mainstream tastes of their friends, no longer had to hold out. Rock and roll was no longer taboo; if Dylan could cross that line, so could they."

The Newport Folk Festival was scheduled for four more years, but now oriented more to traditional performers and crafts, and less popular musicians. Bukka White, Howlin' Wolf, Skip James, Son House, Dock Boggs, along with Ramblin' Jack Elliott, Judy Collins, and Phil Ochs, as well as the pop group the Lovin' Spoonful headlined in 1966. The next year almost a week was devoted to featuring Mother Maybelle Carter, Grandpa Jones, Merle Travis, Judy Collins, Canadian songwriter Gordon Lightfoot, and Arlo Guthrie, the young son of Woody. "The 1968 Newport Folk Festival also seemed to keep its distance from the turbulent center of American youth culture," Wein later explained. This was a time of increasing antiwar activities and a developing counter-culture, particularly in California. But topical songwriters Richie Havens, Arlo Guthrie, Tim Buckley, and a 15-year-old Janis Ian were evident, along with traditional banjo player Buell Kazee, blues star B. B. King, and even Big Brother and the Holding Company with Janis Joplin, a rare appearance by an obvious rock and roll group. The 1969 festival, with a small turnout and financial losses, ended the decade with a number of new faces, including Joni Mitchell, Van Morrison, and James Taylor.

Some festivals hardly lasted as long as Newport, such as the UCLA festival, always devoted to traditional musicians, which collapsed after 1965 because the organizers refused to include rock and roll. The Berkeley festival, on the other hand, developed a more eclectic approach for a time. "1967 approached and we consciously decided to emphasize electric rock music," organizer Barry Olivier later explained. "We

BOB DYLAN AND NEWPORT FOLK FESTIVAL 1965

By the summer of 1965 the Newport Folk Festival, launched in 1959, had become the country's folk music annual showplace, featuring both popular singer/songwriters as well as many traditional black and white musicians. The revival had peaked the previous year and was now less in the public eye, but folk music continued to generate much interest (as well as controversy). Bob Dylan's popularity, initially based on his clever lyrics and political songs, was now taking a turn toward more sensitive and introspective songs, but it was not yet clear if he had begun to chart a completely new course. Dylan's controversial appearance at Newport would forever mark his break with the past and serve as a touchstone for trying to understand the shifting winds of folk music, when electric instrumentation was becoming part of the scene. The Paul Butterfield Blues Band, a racially mixed group from Chicago that played electrified urban blues, was part of the festival's blues workshop, which led to a fight between folklorist Alan Lomax and Albert Grossman, who wanted to be the group's manager. Lomax preferred the traditional African-American musicians to the new group, who received more attention from the young white audience.

The struggle during the blues workshop was a prelude to further controversy during the Sunday evening finale. When the Butterfield Blues Band opened the show some, such as Pete Seeger, festival promoter George Wein, and Lomax, believed that the sound system was inadequate for their electric instruments and the music was inappropriate, while Peter Yarrow defended the band. Dylan appeared later in the evening and surprised the audience by bringing on the stage a backup group that included some members of the Butterfield Blues Band. They played a short set of only three songs: "Maggie's Farm," "Like a Rolling Stone," and "It Takes a Train to Cry." During his set and when he left the stage, there was a loud mixture of cheering and booing. He was prodded to return with an acoustic guitar and performed another new composition, "It's All Over Now, Baby Blue." Some were surely offended by Dylan's new songs and rock styling, while others expected a much longer set and also were unable to hear the lyrics because the sound system could not handle the volume of the electric instruments. Others, certainly, had already heard his newer recordings with electric instruments and, as fans of the Beatles and other rock groups, were open to what would soon be known as folk rock.

Dylan's performance at Newport has echoed through the decades as the defining moment in his life, his turn from folk to rock star. It is also seen as an event that kicked off a vocal, even physical, reaction to his new music. Indeed, soon after during his concert at Forest Hills, near New York City, the crowd yelled "we want the old Dylan," and some even tried to rush the stage during the closing number, "Like a Rolling Stone." *New York Times* music journalist Robert Shelton, who had first praised Dylan in print only a few years earlier, again defended him: "By the time they get to know his excellent new folk rock songs, such as 'Tombstone Blues,' maybe the young boors who ruined an artistically strong concert may have grown up a bit." He was right, and in the United States the criticism quickly died down.

But not in England, where Dylan would receive a somewhat harsh, and infamous, reception. The following spring, at a concert at Manchester's Free Trade Hall, where he was backed by The Hawks, someone in the audience shouted "JUDAS" after Dylan performed "One Too Many Mornings." Student Keith Butler, who received support from others, was angered that Dylan had altered this song into a rock format. Dylan responded, "I don't believe you," and "You're a LIAR!" The bootleg recording of this concert would make history. But Dylan never again faced a hostile crowd, as his music captured a new, and devoted, audience.

arranged to have six electric bands from six different cities," including the Steve Miller Blues Band, Country Joe and the Fish, and Kaleidoscope, along with traditional performers Doc Watson and the Reverend Gary Davis. The next year, as the campus and community became more violent, the festival served as a moderating influence, but it had almost run out of steam. The final festival was held in late 1970, with Pete Seeger, Peggy Seeger and Ewan MacColl, Joan Baez, Big Mama Thornton, Ramblin' Jack Elliott, Big Brother and the Holding Company, and the rock group the Joy of Cooking, perhaps something for everyone. Olivier next devoted his energies to a one-day Berkeley Fiddlers' Convention. On the other hand, the low-key Philadelphia Folk Festival would continue through the century and into the next, a testament to its volunteer staff and consistent lineup of musicians.

Other sorts of music festivals sprang up through the decade. Sarah Gertrude Knott remained head of the National Folk Festival, which struggled through the sixties, moving from location to location in an attempt to retain its audience in competition with so many new festivals. While Ralph Rinzler worked to broaden the Newport festival to include more folk arts, he also proposed a major folk festival in Washington, D.C., which would be more focused yet more expansive than the ongoing National Folk Festival. Rinzler's dream came true in 1967 with the first of the Smithsonian festivals on the Mall, attracting more than half a million visitors. Rinzler featured numerous vernacular performers, including Skip James, the Preservation Jazz Band, Muddy Waters, Grandpa Jones, Doc Watson, and the Georgia Sea Island Singers. In addition to the variety of folk musicians, the festival would always include numerous folk artists working at their crafts.

Folk festivals had a difficult time competing with the proliferating pop and rock festivals through the latter half of the decade. The highly successful Monterey Pop Festival in 1967, for example, featured Simon and Garfunkel, Janis Joplin with Big Brother and the Holding Company, the Butterfield Blues Band, the Jefferson Airplane, the Byrds, Jimi Hendrix, and the Grateful Dead—a showcase for the emerging California rock groups and many others. Ellen Sander in *Sing Out!* praised it for being "a monumental event in every aspect.... Rock was presented, proudly, as an art form, serious but gleeful development of unquestionable talent rather than a fast buck, tennybop curiosity." Other rock festivals followed, capped off by Woodstock in 1969.

FOLK ROCK

The arrival of the Beatles from England in 1964, whose recordings had already been circulating, had an immediate impact on both folk and rock and roll musicians. The growing youth market immediately took to the Beatles and the wave of British groups soon to follow, while the Americans struggled to compete. Bob Dylan was one of many who would switch to the electric guitar and compose songs which were more introspective. He had released the semi-electric album *Bringing It All Back Home* in March 1965, a few months before Newport, which included "Tambourine Man," "Gates of Eden," and "It's All Over Now Baby Blue." The single "Like a Rolling Stone" would reach number two on the pop charts by September. While some were angry at Dylan for not only going electric, but also abandoning his protest songs, the vast majority remained loyal fans, as rock and roll came to dominate the youthful music scene.

Although Dylan's 1965 Newport appearance with an electric guitar appeared to trigger a major controversy, he was not the pioneer in what would quickly become known as folk rock. "It was a crazy-quilt of connective threads between musicians, styles, generations, politics, the record industry, and the mass media," historian Richie Unterberger has explained. "It was envisioned by virtually no one in 1963, yet within two years—after unforeseen thunderbolts such as the JFK [President John F. Kennedy] assassination, the arrival of the Beatles in the United States, the British invasion, and the Byrds drawing overflowing crowds with their folk-based music played on loud electric guitars— folk-rock had overrun the Western world." Unterberger has a difficult time defining exactly what it was, just a "wide umbrella" encompassing all sorts of groups and sounds.

The Animals, a British rock group, who were influenced by the early Dylan, perhaps started things off with their recording of "House of the Rising Sun," which hit the top of the charts in the fall of 1964. "The Animals had transformed a folk lament into a powerhouse rock song," Unterberger explains. Next, a group of folk performers in Los Angeles, including David Crosby, Gene Clark, Chris Hillman, and Jim "Roger" McGuinn formed the Byrds. Their recording of Dylan's "Mr. Tambourine Man" became a hit by early summer 1965, and they quickly followed with "Turn, Turn, Turn," a biblical passage set to music by Pete Seeger, which also scored by year's end. The Byrds would personify folk rock, but they were far from alone. About the same time Barry McGuire recorded P. F. Sloan's antiwar "Eve of Destruction," which climbed to number one, and Simon and Garfunkel's "Sounds of Silence," was also a hit by year's end. "With a dozen more songs of protest snapping close behind, it [Eve of Destruction] heralds a radical change for rock 'n' roll," *Time* announced in mid-September. "Tackling everything from the Peace Corps to the P.T.A., foreign policy to domestic morality, they are sniping away in the name of 'folk rock'—big beat music with big-message lyrics." Folk rock would not be particularly noted for its political messages, but it began in the wake of Dylan's earlier protest stage and easily connected to the political upheavals of the time. "What is happening is that we are into a Combination thing, an Era of Amalgamation, the latest manifestation of which seems to be Folk & Rock & Protest," Boston *Broadside*'s Ed Freeman explained, with some sarcasm. "The idea is to take two dissimilar forms of music, stick 'em together, and ZONK! Instant fame & fortune." Obviously not all were pleased with the new sound.

Dylan had played rock and roll in the fifties, and to some extent he was returning to his high school roots, as were many others, but some had taken a different path. Michael Bloomfield and Paul Butterfield, for example, had grown up on the sounds of Southside Chicago blues. "Muddy Waters, he was like a god to me," Bloomfield would recall. "Well, if he was a god, B. B. King was a deity where I couldn't even imagine ever knowing someone of his magnitude and greatness. But Muddy was in Chicago." He and his friends would sneak into the clubs, but by the age of 17 the versatile Bloomfield was good enough on the guitar to sit in with Muddy's band. "I had played a lot of folk music—stuff like Gary Davis and Doc Watson and [Merle] Travis picking. I was doing this when I was seventeen or eighteen. I was playing acoustic guitar, really a stone folkie. I played with a lot of bluegrass bands and did a lot of country blues," but his real love was urban blues. At the same time Paul Butterfield was learning the harmonica by also hanging around the blues clubs. At the University of Chicago he met Elvin Bishop, a gifted guitar player, and they formed a band. They were performing at a Northside club, where Muddy Waters and Howlin' Wolf also began appearing, and soon became the interracial Butterfield Blues Band with Bishop, Jerome Arnold, Mark Naftalin, Billy Davenport, and Bloomfield. They first recorded for Elektra in 1965. Albert Grossman invited them to Newport, planning on becoming their manager, which brought them together with Dylan. "Going electric didn't mean falsifying anything (any more than acoustic music was a guarantee of integrity), and going electric carried an emotional wallop," Elektra Records owner Jac Holzman has written. "There was greater tonal flexibility, a wider range of shadings. It made an order of magnitude difference. And it was new." He enthusiastically signed John Sebastian and the Lovin' Spoonful as well as the Butterfield Blues Band. The latter was never part of the folk rock movement, except perhaps for its brief appearance with Dylan at Newport that sparked so much controversy. But the band does illustrate another side of the folk movement, its connection to Chess Records and the urban blues revival, which all seemed to blend together by this time.

DECADE ENDS

The record companies had already begun to move away from folk in 1965. Vanguard had issued numerous records from the 1963 and 1964 Newport Folk Festivals, but only one from 1965 (which did not include Dylan). After recording the Butterfield Blues Band, Elektra, now in the process of moving to Los Angeles, recorded the Doors in 1967 and other rock groups. Prestige cancelled its folk department by 1965, and the major labels turned to more lucrative sounds, although folk performers would always find a niche. But there were no longer compilation albums named hootenanny or folk stars. There was scant concern in writing about folk music in the national press by 1965, which was fascinated with rock and roll, but the continuing interest among college students also led to the rapid growth of folklore programs at various universities, including UCLA, Indiana University, the University of Pennsylvania, and the University of Texas. Research and scholarly publications into the history and development of folk songs and dances proliferated.

The decade had been a roller coaster ride for folk music, reaching a peak in 1964, then a swift downhill slide. It had also gone through various sounds and styles, all of which would last into the future, with the singer/songwriters, led by Dylan, the most successful in carrying on a folk tradition that dated from Woody Guthrie. The discovery of so many traditional performers was a stimulating connection between past and present, although many of the older performers would not survive the decade (Frank Proffitt, 1965; Mississippi John Hurt, 1966; Clarence Ashley, 1967; Skip James, 1969), or die soon after (Reverend Gary Davis, Buell Kazee, Dock Boggs, Bukka White). But their recordings, both old reissues and new performances, would bring their music to new generations. There was also the introduction to a wide audience of older musical styles, such as Cajun music from Louisiana. The 1964 Newport Folk Festival included Dewey Balfa and Gladius Thibodeaux, perhaps the first Cajun musicians to appear at a major northern event. The British revival had been less complex, but still retained various strands of folk music, past and present. Traditional songs were mixed with new compositions and performance styles, producing electric folk, the British equivalent of folk rock. All of these trends would continue through the century, including the proliferation of ethnic and world music in the festivals and recording studios.

CENTURY ENDS

GREAT BRITAIN

Following the folk music commercial upsurge and the subsequent general decline of the 1960s, there was increasing confusion over what exactly was "folk music." Grasping for identity or definitions, in 1970 a group of students gathered in Birmingham to discuss the "relationship between the folk arts and contemporary culture." Once engaged, they quickly concluded that there was no simple way that folk enthusiasts could talk any longer of a "folk revival." Even worse, they discovered that "the term 'folk song' had virtually lost its meaning, that the revival had lost most of the pretensions to radicalism that it had once had, and that folk song had been virtually completely co-opted and absorbed by the apathy machines of Tin Pan Alley."

It could hardly be challenged that folk music had lost much of its former oppositional nature. Some were disturbed by the increasing emphasis on instrumental virtuosity, feeling the original emphasis on songs of social change was being lost. Ewan MacColl was bothered by a different situation. "By the seventies," he wrote in his autobiography *Journeyman*, "the revival could boast quite a large number of talented instrumentalists, but of only a handful of skillful singers. And by the eighties that number had dwindled still further. It was with a real sense of shock that we—those of us who had been present at its concept and birth—saw the revival slipping away." Still, there was much that appeared to remain about the same.

Folk music in both Great Britain and the United States was shaped by the same general influences and issues, although there were some differences of emphasis. Most importantly, the understanding and market for folk music were somewhat broadened as the century wound down. For one thing, world music took hold, particularly in the United States, linking musicians (and audiences) from various countries in a greater understanding of diverse backgrounds and cultures. There continued to be a tension (and confusion) between contemporary/popular and vernacular music (which connected with traditional songs and singers), with the latter experiencing somewhat of a revival. Topical/protest songs and musicians continued to perform on both sides of the Atlantic, although with less public presence than had existed in the 1960s. The changing technology of musical reproduction—with the appearance of compact discs (CDs)—and easier distribution—through the Internet—made all sorts of folk music, old and new, readily available.

CLUBS AND FESTIVALS

According to Niall Mackinnon, in his book *The British Folk Scene* (1994), by the seventies folk music was "performed in folk clubs, folk festivals, sessions, singarounds, dances, ceilidhs [an informal concert form], [formal] concerts, the street, pub rooms, private parties, and so on." Most important were the clubs and festivals. The 300 folk clubs in Great

Britain in the mid-1960s had grown to perhaps more than 1,000 within a decade, and about 500 were still around in the mid-1980s. The clubs were locally controlled and often specialized in regional and traditional music. The specialized "singers" clubs included only the performers, a circumstance that worried MacColl: "The folk boom had created a situation where there were more clubs than there were resident performers, and club organisers were competing with each other for the services of so-called 'stars.' A star was anyone who had been on the folk-club touring circuit for more than a year." Many of the clubs attempted to preserve traditional musical forms, which historian Michael Brocken has criticized as being out of touch with the modern world: "The folk club coterie of the 1970s transformed the folk revival by acting out a fantasy of authenticity that their own time denied them." He argued that the "folk clubs became self-absorbed in a passion, that the musical authentic could be relocated…. Many folkies come to appreciate 'their' music by basing their tastes on what they and their listening colleagues discerned to know already rather than what they were willing to learn—a musical cul-de-sac." Ewan MacColl's approach had seemingly captured most of the clubs, with perhaps unfortunate results, according to some.

If many of the clubs were perhaps too inbred and insular, a self-contained world clinging to inauthentic tradition—though club and audience members certainly did not think so—the numerous folk festivals countered with a wide variety of performers and styles. The Cambridge Folk Festival lasted through the century, always presenting a wide range of performers, similar to the Newport festival in the United States. "Rock festivals had degenerated into aggro, beer cans, and gristly hamburgers, but Cambridge delivered what they promised, and if the sweet scent of marijuana was as strong as the malt and hops in the beer tent, then this was just a reflection of its time," festival historians Dave Laing and Richard Newman remarked about the 1970 event. The roster of well-known artists who appeared that year included Pentangle, Martin Carthy, and John Renbourn, as well as Mike Seeger and Stefan Grossman from the United States. There were additional Americans the following year—Rev. Gary Davis, Mimi Farina, and Jean Ritchie—along with the British folk-rock group Steeleye Span and various British musicians. The festivals continued with an eclectic mix, sometimes with electric folk bands, Celtic performers, traditional musicians, and always with at least a few visiting Americans. World music—performers and styles from around the world—had become part of the folk scene in the 1980s, but were slow to make an appearance in Cambridge. West African blues guitarist Ali Farka Toure and S. E. Rogie, a singer and guitarist from Sierra Leone joined Nanci Griffith, the Dillards, and others in 1989. But world music would be hard to find on the program for the remainder of the century.

Other festivals had a similar approach to folk music, mixing older and newer performers, from both sides of the Atlantic, with a concentration on popular acts. "The folk music festival has become an extremely important feature of folk music activity in this country," Michael Brocken argued. "It has matured into possibly the best medium for presenting the eclectic and idiosyncratic in folk music, whilst at the same time drawing attention to the folk scene as an important feeder network." The Lincoln Folk Festival in 1971, for example, headlined Steeleye Span, Dave Swarbrick and Martin Carthy, the Byrds, James Taylor, and Sonny Terry and Brownie McGhee. The English Folk Dance and Song Society (EFDSS) had launched the strictly traditional music Keel Festival in 1965; it was cancelled in 1981 due to a lack of interest, but was revived in 1984 as the National Folk Festival. There were also festivals in Beverly, Warwick, and elsewhere, including Scotland, where the Edinburgh Folk Festival lasted until 2000. The festivals became part of the democratic nature of folk music, attracting a wide range of fans.

Protest/topical songs, including those about world peace, had a long history, which did not dry up, although were perhaps less known as the century wound down. In 1973, the British Peace Committee sponsored a festival at Royal Festival Hall with The Boys of the Lough, the Albion Country Band, and Richard Thompson. Among the most prolific of radical performers was Leon Rosselson, born in 1934, who wrote satirical songs for the TV show *That Was the Week That Was* in the early 1960s. A prolific songwriter and performer, and political activist, he recorded numerous albums, including *If I Knew Who the Enemy Was* (1979). Billy Bragg, born in 1957, began with a punk band, but he soon turned toward a folk style, joining Richard Thompson, among others. He wrote numerous topical songs, including "The Milkman of Human Kindness," "A New England" (a hit for Kirsty MacColl, daughter of Ewan), and "The Man in the Iron Mask." In the 1980s he supported labor strikes and joined Labour MPs in the "Jobs for Youth" tour. He later appeared, backed by the American group Wilco, on two commercially successful CDs of unpublished Woody Guthrie poems, for which they wrote or adapted the music.

Electric folk groups had appeared in concerts and festivals, but they always seemed to be regrouping and vanishing. "Despite the large variety of approaches and possibilities," the author of their history, Britta Sweers, has summed up, "the electric folk direction seemed to have come to a dead end by the late 1970s." Pentangle folded in 1972, Fairport Convention broke up in 1979, about the same time that Steeleye Span disbanded, but they all reformed from time to time. Other groups, however, faced a permanent demise. Electric folk could not compete with newer musical styles, such as punk, disco, new wave, or funk. Still, many

MIKE SEEGER

Mike Seeger was born in 1933, the eldest of the four children born to Charles and Ruth Crawford Seeger, and the half-brother of Pete. Growing up in a musical family near Washington, D.C., he early began to master a variety of instruments, including the banjo, fiddle, mandolin, and guitar. Unlike Pete, Mike was mostly drawn to southern string band music, and in addition to his skills as a performer he early began to record traditional musicians, and issued the bluegrass album *American Banjo* on Folkways (1956). He recorded the African-American guitarist and singer Elizabeth "Libba" Cotten for Folkways Records in 1957, whom he had met when she worked for his family. In 1958, he joined John Cohen and Tom Paley to form the New Lost City Ramblers, the first of the northern string bands that resurrected old-time music for a modern audience, which they learned from old 78 records and Harry Smith's *Anthology of American Folk Music*. Their first album for Folkways quickly followed, as did about one a year into the 1960s, including such titles as *American Moonshine and Prohibition Songs* (1963). Tracey Schwartz replaced Paley in 1962. According to the *Music Hound Folk: The Essential Album Guide* (1998): "The Ramblers' influence

of the musicians continued to record and perform. Fairport Convention played a reunion concert in the Oxfordshire town of Cropredy in 1980, which became the site of an annual three-day festival. Drawing large crowds, the festival featured electric folk bands. "Around the middle of the late 1980s, with the emergence of new independent recording labels, major groups such as Pentangle, Steeleye Span, and Fairport Convention started to reassemble, although often as part-time bands, and to record again," Sweers concludes. "The electric folk movement of the 1960s and 1970s has now acquired a cult status as a model for other contemporary approaches to folk music. This is the case not only in other European countries but also in the United States, which originally supplied the models for the British on generations of young musicians who have followed in their footsteps is incalculable; it's difficult to imagine a revival of old-time music of any consequence without them."

The Ramblers appeared at numerous festivals and continued their recording through the 1960s, after which they basically went their separate ways, although the group continued to be regrouped from time to time into the next century. Various compilation CD albums have been issued by Smithsonian Folkways Recordings as well as Rounder, with *Forty Years of Concert Performances* (2000). In the meantime, Mike Seeger kept up a busy performance and recording schedule, for example *Oldtime Country Music* (1962), *Tipple, Loom, and Rail* (1965), *Mike and Peggy Seeger* (1966), *The Second Annual Farewell Reunion* (1973), *The Third Annual Farewell Reunion* (1994), and many others. He produced a documentary film on southern step dancing in the '80s. He continued to explore old-time music and dance, for example in his album *Mike Seeger: Fresh Oldtime String Band Music* (1988) and continued recording through the next decade, for example *Way Down in North Carolina* (1996). Into the twenty-first century, he continued his prolific and influential career of performing and presenting traditional music to the world.

revival and electric folk scenes." The advent of CDs made their old and new recordings readily available.

THE UNITED STATES

The folk scene in the United States for the rest of the century became extremely complex, going off in directions that could hardly be anticipated in 1970 when the Newport Folk Festival collapsed. Some observers speculated that perhaps all modern music was folk music. "A slow but dramatic metamorphosis in contemporary musical expression is transforming most 'popular' music into 'folk music,'" Gene Youngblood argued in the *Lost Angeles Free Press* in 1967. "The young generation is a generation of plug-in troubadours. Slung over their back is an electric fuzz bass instead

U. UTAH PHILLIPS

Among the myriad modern folk performers and song writers, Bruce "U. Utah" Phillips has been one of the most colorful and creative. Born in Cleveland, Ohio, in 1935, the son of left-wing parents, he early began traveling around with bums and hobos before serving with the Army during the Korea War in the early 1950s. For the next few decades, he worked as a union activist and social worker in Utah, having joined the radical Industrial Workers of the World (IWW), and he relished union songs such as "Solidarity Forever" and Joe Hill's "Power in the Union." He had early learned the guitar and begun writing songs, and recorded his first album, *Nobody Knows Me*, on the Prestige label in the early 1960s, but did not become a professional folk musician until the late 1970s. He next released *Welcome to Caffe Lena*, which was followed by a stream of albums for Rounder/Philo, Red House, and other labels through the 1990s, including some with creative colleagues. For example, he appeared on the *Legends of Folk* album with Spider John Koerner and Ramblin' Jack Elliott, and *The Long Memory* with Rosalie Sorrels. The punk/folk star

of a homemade lute…. And because of them it is increasingly true: 'pop' music is 'folk' music, from Beatles to Baez to Dylan and Donovan." While folk music was no longer recognized as a commercial wonder, it remained very much part of the country's musical landscape, but now dominated by the singer/songwriters who had become a vital part of the folk revival in the 1960s.

Forty years later, Boston folk music journalist Scott Alarik asked in late 2000, "Is the singer–songwriter revival over? Beginning in the mid-1980s, a bumper crop of songwriters grew from coffeehouses to national stardom, beginning with Bill Morrissey, Patty Larkin, and Greg Brown, followed by the even greater commercial success of Nanci Griffith, Suzanne Vega, John Gorka, and Shawn Colvin. The wave only grew in the '90s, with the convincing local climbs of the Story, Ellis Paul, Martin Sexton, and Catie

Ani DiFranco recorded his songs on her album *The Past Didn't Go Anywhere*, and they also collaborated on *Fellow Workers*. He kept up an active performing schedule until health issues forced his semi-retirement at century's end.

Phillips has been a prolific songwriter, and his songs have been extensively recorded. Counted among his best are "I Remember Loving You," "Starlight on the Rails," The Telling Takes Me Home," "The Goodnight-Loving Trail," "Daddy, What's a Train?", and "All Used Up." He is just as effective when describing personal relationships, labor heroes, the disappearance of passenger railroads, historical events, the oppressive nature of poverty, the horrors of warfare, or old friends. He released his songbook *Starlight on the Rails and Other Songs* (1973). A four-disc audio-songbook appeared in 2005, *Starlight on the Rails*, summing up Phillips's musical and activist life through dozens of songs and recorded thoughts—he is also a wonderful storyteller—on Daemon Records. Utah Phillips, self-styled "The Golden Voice of the Great Southwest," well captured the connection between folk music and personal politics/commitment through the second half of the twentieth century.

Curtis, and a spate of national folk-pop stars, cresting with Jewel's 1996 break to Madonna-like superstardom and the blockbuster 1997 Lilith Fair tour of women songwriters launched by Sarah McLachlan." Alarik's concern over the seeming recent demise of promising singer/songwriters captured only a part, although an important part, of the folk music world that had emerged over the past few decades.

The 1970s were a testing time for traditional folk music, a time to regroup and adjust to a world in which what some called "roots" music had scant popular recognition. Some of the better organized and promoted festivals continued, such as Philadelphia and at the University of Chicago, while others vanished. The Newport Folk Festival was revived in 1985 and, with various sponsors, would continue through the remainder of the century and into the next. The National Folk Festival, now under the leadership of the

National Council of Traditional Arts, continued its annual gatherings, moving the location every few years. Rod Kennedy started the Kerrville (Texas) Folk Festival in 1972, with a focus on such Texas musicians as Carolyn Hester, Mance Lipscomb, and John Lomax, Jr. The festival would grow over the decades into a major national event. Scores of more specialized festivals dotted the landscape, representing every sort of folk music style and musical contest; there were, for example, dozens of bluegrass festivals.

Sing Out! and some other folk magazines managed to survive, but many others had short lives. The *Little Sandy Review*, for example, collapsed in the mid-1960s. After struggling for many years, *Broadside* finally ceased publication in 1988. However, some new magazines emerged on the local level. *Come For to Sing* was founded in 1975 in Chicago in conjunction with the Old Town School of Folk Music. It had a particular focus: "traditional music, blues, Appalachian music, bluegrass, reissues and old-time music, the Chicago folk music scene, instrumental styles, and folk music resources." *Dirty Linen*, a national rival to *Sing Out!*, began appearing in the 1980s, first as a newsletter for fans of Fairport Convention and similar folk-rock groups. It expanded to being a major voice for world music performers. *No Depression* began in the 1990s to reflect the "Americana" wing of the singer/songwriter movement, while more specializing publications, including the long-running *Banjo Newsletter* and the *Old-Time Herald*, covered specific areas of interest in the folk community.

One of the significant developments was the rise of women's folk music, including festivals and record labels. After leaving a promising acting career, Holly Near became a folk performer and issued her first album in 1973 on her own label, Redwood Records (simultaneously with the founding of Olivia Records, another women's music label). She was a pioneer in women's music, with a heavy political orientation, including promoting gay rights. She appeared at the

National Women's Music Festival in Champaign-Urbana, Illinois, in 1976, a few years after it was started by Kristin Lems, another activist folk musician. "The festival organizers were excited that I had agreed to attend," Near has explained. "Kristen was not only involved in the women's movement, she was a world-view peace activist. My music represented a holistic perspective." The first Michigan Women's Music Festival occurred soon after, with Near also appearing, along with Meg Christian and other gay/feminist singer/songwriters, such as Cris Williamson and Margie Adam. Such festivals proliferated, such as the San Diego Women's Music Festival, demonstrating the continuity as well as fragmenting of the folk music world. Ani DiFranco launched her Righteous Babe Records in 1990 to release her own records, and quickly became a major musical figure with a wide following, particularly among young women. Sweet Honey in the Rock, an African-American women's group formed in 1973 by Bernice Johnson Reagon, an original member of the Freedom Singers, linked gospel, freedom songs, blues, rap, African songs, and much more.

WORLD MUSIC

Folk music from around the world had been part of the revival since the 1950s, but became a significant aspect during the remaining decades of the century. *Sing Out!* had long covered music from Mexico, Eastern Europe, and certainly the British Isles, but by the early 1990s it began to explore a much broader geographical scope. In early 1993, *Sing Out!* published an article on Mahlathini and the Mahotella Queens, a South African township musical group, soon followed by a piece on the widely popular Ladysmith Black Mambazo. The Weavers had had a hit with "Wimoweh" 40 years earlier, originally written by the South African Solomon Linda, as had the pop group the Tokens with their version, called "The Lion Sleeps Tonight," which had risen to number one on the music charts in 1962. But music from South Africa, and Africa in general, was hardly known in the United States until near the century's end. Paul Simon featured Ladysmith Black Mambazo and the Senegalese singer Youssou N'Dour on his popular album *Graceland* (1986). He toured with South African exiles Hugh Masekela and Miriam Makeba in 1987.

Soon thereafter, *Sing Out!* featured an article on Peru's Huayno music, as documented by John Cohen (a member of the old-time group New Lost City Ramblers). Cohen's fascination with southern traditional string-band music had spurred him to find a traditional style in the Andes in the early 1960s. The following issue found the blues journalist and historian Elijah Wald exploring the music of Tarika Sammy from Madagascar. Next appeared a piece on Boukman Eksperyans from Haiti, and the floodgates were opened.

During this same period Grateful Dead drummer Mickey Hart and Alan Jabbour, director of the American Folklife Center at the Library of Congress, initiated the Endangered Music Project to preserve the world's ethnic music, and to be distributed on the Rykodisc label—a modern version of Alan Lomax's earlier series of world recordings and Moe Asch's impressive output on Folkways Records. Hart's researches later appeared in *Song Catchers: In Search of the World's Music* (2003). *Sing Out!* also covered musical groups from India, Senegal, Mali, Mongolia, and various other countries. World music began appearing on radio shows, at various folk festivals, and in concert halls. The North American Folk Music and Dance Alliance was organized in 1990 to pull together all facets of the folk music community—performers and their agents, journalists, radio show hosts, club owners, record company representatives, instrument makers, and so many others—and at its annual gatherings there was an increasing presence of musicians from throughout the world. "By the 1990s collaborations between American and foreign musicians had become more common," Larry

Starr and Christopher Waterman note in their informative survey *American Popular Music*, "spurred on the one hand by folk and alternative music fans' search for a broader range of musical experiences, and on the other by the globalization of the music industry." There were also political overtones to the popularity of world music, with many searching for greater understanding and sharing in a world full of conflict and exploitation, seemingly despite (or because of) the demise of the Cold War.

While world music was rapidly gathering an audience, stretching the definition and scope of folk music in complex directions, it was joined by a renewed interest in more homegrown sounds. Klezmer music, originally from Eastern Europe and commercially recorded in the 1920s, now made a comeback, led by old-time musician Henry Sapoznik. Creole and Cajun music had a large following, with some of the older recording groups joined by numerous younger musicians. Texas–Mexican and other musical styles from the borderlands joined the new mix, along with Celtic bands and so much else. The range and variety of music by century's end seemed boundless. But the real surprise was the sudden popularity of southern roots music.

SOUTHERN ROOTS MUSIC REVIVAL

The Smithsonian Institution had acquired Folkways Records following Moe Asch's death in 1986 and had continued to make available all of the Folkways record catalog, as well issue new recordings from its vast inventory. In 1997 Smithsonian Folkways Recordings reissued Harry Smith's *Anthology of American Folk Music* in a large CD box, with both original and new liner notes. The *Anthology* quickly generated enormous sales and numerous Grammy awards, a surprise to all involved, and an indication that traditional music was certainly not without commercial appeal. Various specialized labels had been issuing limited-run CDs of roots recordings from the 1920s to 1930s, particularly including the German label Bear Family Records, but this was the first indication that a mass audience existed, particularly among young people who had grown up on the latest of rock and rap. At the same time, in their increasingly infrequent reunion concerts, the New Lost City Ramblers kept the flame of old-time music alive, but they could hardly have anticipated such a mass market for the music they had pioneered 40 years earlier.

Perhaps the Harry Smith reissue could be considered a fluke, but just a few years later, in 2000, the popular movie *O Brother, Where Art Thou?* demonstrated that roots music had a definite mass appeal. The soundtrack included an actual field recording, Alan Lomax's prison recording in 1959 of "Po Lazarus," and included various contemporary musicians doing older songs, such as Ralph Stanley's "Oh Death," Norman Blake's "I Am a Man of Constant Sorrow," and Alison Krauss's "Down to the River to Pray." The soundtrack CD immediately shot up the charts, selling more than four million, though it was not played on any commercial country music radio stations, and garnered five Grammy awards, including Album of the Year. "Down From the Mountain," a concert in Nashville's Ryman Auditorium in May 2000, featured some of the same performers from the movie soundtrack—John Hartford, Alison Krauss and Union Station, the Cox Family, Gillian Welch, and Emmylou Harris— which resulted in its own CD and a successful national tour.

All of this was a fulfillment of journalist Alex Abramovich's 1998 prediction of such a broad, receptive audience. Abramovich wrote, "If America's fascination with folk music faded a quarter century ago, joining pet rocks, hula hoops, and other 'crazes' in an imaginary museum of the American mind, stirrings suggest that, while nothing resembling a 'movement' is afoot, pockets of resurgent interest exist... . While the absence of any coherent

ROUNDER RECORDS

In 1970, three Cambridge, Massachusetts college students, Bill Nowlin, Marian Leighton-Levy, and Ken Irwin, beginning with their love for folk music but few resources, launched Rounder Records. They started with an interest in southern old-time, bluegrass, and blues music, and by century's end they had issued more than 3,000 albums that also included world, soul, socas, jazz, juju, Cajun, Celtic, rhythm and blues, reggae, and singer/songwriters. They became the largest independent label in the country. Old-time banjo player George Pegram appeared on their first album, followed by the guitar genius Norman Blake, the bluegrass group J. D. Crowe and the New South, and other southern instrumentalists. "It was the fiery blues-rock stylings of [George] Thorogood—which, while pumped up with electricity, were rooted in the sincerity and integrity that marks all Rounder artists—that put Rounder on the map internationally," the owners have written. They followed with reissues of early recordings as well as contemporary artists such as Ricky Skaggs, Tony Trischka, Tony Rice, Clarence "Gatemouth" Brown, and D. L. Menard.

Rounder's purchase of Philo Records in 1984 brought it singer/songwriter Nanci Griffith, as well as Utah Phillips, Dave Van Ronk, Christine Lavin, and other performers. They signed the teenage Alison Krauss, whose first album in 1987 launched her spectacular bluegrass/country career. Rounder took on the responsibility in the 1990s of issuing the massive Alan Lomax Collection, which will eventually include more than 100 CDs of the folklorist's field recordings and much else from his long career. They had already issued the three volumes of Lomax's Library of Congress interviews of Lead Belly, and have pursued other joint projects with the Library of Congress Archive of Folk Culture. In addition to including the Philo label, they also obtained the Flying Fish label, filling their catalog with numerous contemporary folk artists, such as John Hartford and the Red Clay Ramblers. By the twenty-first century the original owners were still in charge, having created a musical organization that preserved the best of the older sounds as well as featuring numerous younger musicians, from around the world. It well represented the eclectic definition of folk music at century's end.

'movement' prohibits drawing straight lines between artists and writers spearheading a '90s folk revival... , it does seem that stages are being set, and audiences primed, in such a way that if the ghosts of old-time musicians were to walk upon them again, they might be sure, for the first time, of a reception unadorned by politics." Something was definitely happening. The feature film *Songcatcher*, released in 2000 and featuring derivative-folk musicians Taj Mahal and Iris DeMent, was based on the story of a northern folklorist discovering and recording ballads in the early twentieth century Appalachians. While not as commercially successful as *O Brother, Where Art Thou?*, it received critical attention. Old-time music bands began to flourish throughout the country, with names such as the Crooked Jades, Ollabelle, the Duhks, the Reeltime Travelers, Uncle Earl, and the Mammals. Banjo and acoustic guitar sales have steadily increased, as have old-time festivals and informal gatherings (although outnumbered by the bluegrass festivals).

In conjunction with the rebirth of country roots music, there was also an acoustic blues revival, particularly drawing upon Mississippi Delta musical ancestors. While Taj Mahal had long carried the banner for acoustic blues in the folk music world, a host of younger musicians, including Corey Harris, Alvin Youngblood Hart, Keb' Mo', Guy Davis, and Chris Thomas (who appeared on the *O Brother* soundtrack) took up the cause. These and other younger blues musicians have since attracted a sizeable following and notable record sales.

Perhaps the fascination with roots music was summed up with the multipart *American Roots Music* (Santelli et al. 2001) documentary that appeared on PBS stations throughout the country in 2001. There ensued DVDs, as well as companion CDs and a large book. "In the past quarter century, interest in American roots music has risen dramatically," the book's editor Robert Santelli explains. "Festivals featuring various roots music forms occur across the country every spring, summer, and fall. The Chicago Blues Festival alone draws more than one hundred thousand fans to Grant Park, on the shores of Lake Michigan, each June. In New Orleans, the city's annual Jazz and Heritage Festival attracts an equal number of roots music lovers to its fairgrounds and clubs. Fiddlers' conventions in the Carolinas, folk festivals in New Jersey, and Pennsylvania, and Native American powwows on reservations, back east and out west, not only celebrate American roots music in the twenty-first century but also help one to preserve our rich music heritage—despite the increasing encroachments of cultural homogenization." The documentary series and book cover not only early and contemporary blues, country, and gospel music, but also Cajun and zydeco, Tejano (from Mexican Texas), Native American, and even rock and roll. This was a broad approach, though much was necessarily omitted.

THE CENTURY ENDS

Folk music had taken on various identifications and aspects by century's end. Some wondered what had happened to topical songs/protest music, however, which had previously been a vital part of folk, particularly in the 1930s and again in the 1960s. In a 2000 article in *Acoustic Guitar*, David Simons presented a brief history of protest music and explored its current difficulties. "In the late '70s, apathy eventually made room for a new crusade with the arrival of the antinuclear movement—yet the musical response was often labored," he argues. "Near the end of the '80s, the subtlety and simplicity that was the hallmark of prime protest music finally resurfaced in a series of songs about domestic violence and economic hardship. The trend began with "Luka," Suzanne Vega's moving tale about a battered urban child." Simons also notes Tracy Chapman's "Fast Car," about urban poverty, and Neil Young's "Rockin' in the Free World," on domestic blight, the numerous songs of Steve Earle, such as "Christmas in Washington," Ani DiFranco, and Bruce Springsteen. While Bob Dylan was no longer considered a protest singer, he would usually perform some of his earlier songs in concerts. Pete Seeger continued to present old and new songs about civil rights, world peace, poverty, pollution, and so much more. Protest songs would remain part of folk music, but only as one aspect of a much larger musical scene.

Since Dylan had turned from politics to personal matters in the midsixties, singer/songwriters had generally followed suit, focusing on individual issues and introspection. To assist in getting their music distributed, a group in Greenwich Village, including Dave Van Ronk, began *The Fast Folk Musical Magazine* in early 1982, with each issue including an album. Somewhat more than 100 issues appeared until it folded in 1997, including more than 1,000 songs. Smithsonian Folkways Recordings produced a two-CD *Fast Folk* retrospective in 2002. "The great community of songwriters in New York's Greenwich Village, who took their writing seriously, who considered what they did an art form, needed to draw attention to itself," Jack Hardy, *Fast Folk's* creator, explains. While Greenwich Village appeared to continue to represent the center of folk music, by century's end there was no longer a commercial folk club in the community, although folk music, in all of its forms, flourished throughout the city. Indeed, since the 1960s the number of folk clubs drastically declined nationwide, with concert halls and the scores of festivals having taken their place in the presentation of performers. Singer/songwriters continued to proliferate. Indeed, with the coming of CD technology and the Internet, it had become quite efficient to produce and market albums, bypassing the major record companies and expensive commercial advertising. There are now dozens of small labels specializing in folk and roots music.

By century's end, there was also a vast array of published studies to assist in understanding the previous two centuries and more of folk music's development in Great Britain and the United States. In addition to the various biographies and autobiographies—Bob Dylan, Pete Seeger, Woody Guthrie, Lead Belly, the Carter Family, Jimmie Rodgers, John Lomax, and Ewan MacColl—there have also been numerous interpretative studies and accounts of seemingly every conceivable aspect of folk music. Moreover, there are documentary films giving a graphic visual understanding of the musicians, songs, and other relevant topics. Today we can listen to and understand folk music's past and present, a rich treasure of sounds. The 78th Mountain Dance and Folk Festival was held in Asheville, North Carolina, in 2005, featuring acoustic performances of southern music, one indication of musical continuity. Rapidly changing technology makes available a century's worth of recorded sounds, a gold mine of music that brings folk music, in all of its styles and forms, into every home and computer. Folk music has been shared by the people for centuries and this will continue. Folk music has never been easy to define, but it has always existed, and always will, in some form or fashion.

DISCOGRAPHY

This discography is limited to compilation folk music albums that have been issued in CD format, and that are hopefully currently available, as well as a few representing individual groups and performers.

The Alan Lomax Collection: Sampler (1997) 1 CD. Rounder Records CD PR 1700.

American Roots: A History of American Folk Music (1999) 4 CDs. Disky CB248572.

American Roots Music (2001) 4 CDs. Palm Pictures.

Anthology of American Folk Music (1997) 6 CDs. Smithsonian Folkways Recordings.

Arhoolie Records 40th Anniversary Collection, 1960–2000: The Journey of Chris Strachwitz (2000) 5 CDs. Arhoolie Productions CD491.

As Good As It Gets: Skiffle (2000) 2 CDs. As Good As It Gets 25052.

A Taste of Tradition, Vol. 3 (1996) 1 CD. Tradition VCD 1003.

A Treasury of Library of Congress Field Recordings (1997) 1 CD. Rounder Records CD 1500.

The Best of Broadside, 1962–1988: Anthems of the American Underground From the Pages of Broadside Magazine (2000) 5 CDs. Smithsonian Folkways Recordings SFW CD 40130.

Back to the Crossroads: The Roots of Robert Johnson (2004) 1 CD. Yazoo 2070.

Billy Bragg & Wilco, *Mermaid Avenue* (1998) 1 CD. Elektra 62204-2.

Bleecker Street: Greenwich Village in the 60s (1999) 1 CD. Astor Place Recordings TCD4012.

Bob Dylan, *The Bootleg Series, Vol. 1–3* (1991) 3 CDs. Columbia C3K 65302.

The Bristol Sessions, Vol. 1 (2002) 1 CD. RCA/BMG Heritage 07863651312.

Classic Bluegrass from Smithsonian Folkways (2002) 1 CD. Smithsonian Folkways Recordings SFW CD 40092.

Classic Mountain Songs from Smithsonian Folkways (2002) 1 CD. Smithsonian Folkways Recordings SFW CD 40094.

Classic Old-Time Music from Smithsonian Folkways (2003) 1 CD. Smithsonian Folkways Recordings SFW CD 40093.

Dave Van Ronk, *The Mayor of MacDougal Street, Rarities 1957–1969* (2005) 1 CD. Lyrichord Discs MCM 4005.

Doughboys, Playboys and Cowboys: The Golden Years of Western Swing (1999) 4 CDs. Proper Records Properbox 6.

Down from the Mountain (2001) 1 CD. Lost Highway 088170221-2.

Down in the Basement: Joe Bussard's Treasure Trove of Vintage 78s, 1926–1937 (2002) 1 CD. Old Hat CD-1004.

The Easy Riders: Marianne (1995) 6 CDs. Bear Family Records BCD 15780.

Fast Folk: A Community of Singers & Songwriters (2002) 2 CDs. Smithsonian Folkways Recordings SFW CD 40135.

Folk Song America: A 20th Century Revival (1990) 4 CDs. Smithsonian Collection of Recordings RD 046.

The Folk Years: A Singers and Songwriters Collection (2002) 8 CDs. Time Life Music R159-29.

Freedom Is a Constant Struggle: Songs of the Mississippi Civil Rights Movement (1994) 2 CDs. Folk Era Records 1419D.

Goodbye, Babylon: Living, Stirring, Sacred Songs, Odes and Anthems, Both New and Old (2003) 6 CDs. Dust-to-Digital DTD-01.

Harry Belafonte: Island in the Sun (2002) 5 CDs. Bear Family Records BCD 16262.

Harry Smith's Anthology of American Folk Music, Vol. 4 (2000) 2 vols. Revenant RVN 211.

Jimmie Rodgers: The Singing Brakeman (1992) 6 CDs. Bear Family Records BCD 15540.

Joan Baez: Rare, Live & Classics (1993) 3 CDs. Vanguard Records 125/27-2.

Kingston Trio: The Guard Years (1997) 10 CDs. Bear Family Records BCD 16160.

Kingston Trio: The Stewart Years (1997) 10 CDs. Bear Family Records BCD 16161.

Leadbelly: King of the 12-String Guitar (1991) 1 CD. Columbia/Legacy CK46776.

Lonnie Donegan: More Than 'Pye in the Sky' (1993) 8 CDs. Bear Family Records BCD 15700.

New Lost City Ramblers: There Ain't No Way Out (1997) 1 CD. Smithsonian Folkways SF CD 40098.

O Brother, Where Art Thou? (2000) 1 CD. Lost Highway 088170-069-2 DGO2.

The Paramount Masters (2003) 4 CDs. JSP Records JSP7723D.

Pete Seeger, *A Link in the Chain* (1996) 2 CDs. Columbia/Legacy C2K 64772.

Peter, Paul and Mary: Carry It On (2003) 4 CDs. Warner Bros. Records R273907.

Phil Ochs: Farewells & Fantasies (1997) 3 CDs. Elektra R273518.

Philadelphia Folk Festival: 40th Anniversary (2001) 4 CDs. Sliced Bread SB74440SL.

The Prestige/Folklore Years, Volume One: All Kinds of Folks (1994) 1 CD. Prestige/Folklore Records PRCD-9901-2.

Philadelphia Folk Festival: Singing Out Loud (1994) 1 CD. Prestige/Folklore Records PRCD-9904-2.

Songs For Political Action: Folkmusic, Topical Songs and the American Left, 1926–1953 (1996) 10 CDs. Bear Family Records BCD 15720.

Song Links 2: A Celebration of English Traditional Songs and Their American Variants (2005) 2 CDs. Fellside.Recordings FECD 190D.

The Real Music Box: 25 Years of Rounder Records (1995) 9 CDs. Rounder Records CD AN25.

The Rose & the Briar: Death, Love and Liberty in the American Ballad (2004) 1 CD. Columbia/Legacy CK92866.

U. Utah Phillips (2005) *Starlight on the Rails: A Songbook.* AK Press AKA041CD.

Vanguard: Collector's Edition (1997) 4 CDs. Vanguard Records, 163/66-2.

Vanguard: Roots of Folk (2002) 3 CDs. Vanguard Records, 203/05-2.

Washington Square Memoirs: The Great Urban Folk Boom, 1950–1970 (2001) 3 CDs. Rhino R274264.

The Weavers, 1949–1953 (2000) 4 CDs. Bear Family Records BCD 15930.

The Weavers: Wasn't That a Time (1993) 4 CDs. Vanguard Records VCD4-147/50.

Where Have All the Flowers Gone: The Songs of Pete Seeger (1998) 2 CDs. Appleseed Recordings 1024.

Woody Guthrie, *This Land Is Your Land: The Asch Recordings, Vol. 1* (1997a) 1 CD. Smithsonian Folkways 40100.

Woody Guthrie, *Muleskinner Blues: The Asch Recordings, Vol. 2* (1997b) 1 CD. Smithsonian Folkways 40101.

Woody Guthrie, *Hard Travelin': The Asch Recordings, Vol. 3* (1998) 1 CD. Smithsonian Recordings 40102.

Woody Guthrie, *Buffalo Skinners: The Asch Recordings, Vol. 4* (1999) 1 CD. Smithsonian Folkways 40103.

BIBLIOGRAPHY

This bibliography is limited to books published in English. Many are still in print, and all should be available in school and public libraries. Many have their own helpful bibliographies that will contain references to published articles, manuscript collections, and other valuable folk music sources.

Abrahams, Roger D. *Singing the Master: The Emergence of African American Culture in the Plantation South.* New York: Pantheon Books, 1992.

Alarik, Scott. *Deep Community: Adventures in the Modern Folk Underground.* Cambridge: Black Wolf Press, 2003.

Altschuler, Glenn C. *All Shook Up: How Rock 'N' Roll Changed America.* New York: Oxford University Press, 2003.

American Folklife Center: An Illustrated Guide. Washington: Library of Congress, 2004.

Baez, Joan. *And a Voice to Sing With: A Memoir.* New York: Summit Books, 1987.

Baggelaar, Kristin, and Donald Milton. *Folk Music: More Than a Song.* New York: Thomas Y. Crowell Company, 1976.

Bastin, Bruce. *Red River Blues: The Blues Tradition in the Southeast.* Urbana: University of Illinois Press, 1986.

Bealle, John. *Old-Time Music and Dance: Community and Folk Revival.* Bloomington: Indiana University Press, 2005.

Becker, Jane S. *Appalachia and the Construction of an American Folk, 1930–1940*. Chapel Hill: University of North Carolina Press, 1998.

Bikel, Theodore. *Theo: The Autobiography of Theodore Bikel*. New York: HarperCollins Publishers, 1994.

Bird, Brian. *Skiffle: The Story of Folk Song with a Jazz Beat*. London: Robert Hale, 1958.

Blake, Benjamin, Jack Rubeck, and Allan Shaw, eds. *The Kingston Trio On Record*. Naperville: Kingston Korner, 1985.

Bogdanov, Vladimir, Chris Woodstra, and Stephen Thomas Erlewine, eds. *All Music Guide to the Blues*. San Francisco: Backbeat Books, 2003.

Bohlman, Philip V. "Immigrant, Folk, and Regional Musics in the Twentieth Century." In *The Cambridge History of American Music*, edited by David Nicholls, pp. 276–308. Cambridge: Cambridge University Press, 1998.

Bookbinder, David. *What Folk Music Is All About*. New York: Julian Messner, 1979.

Boyes, Georgina. *The Imagined Village: Culture, Ideology and the English Folk Revival*. Manchester: Manchester University Press, 1993.

Brand, Oscar. *The Ballad Mongers: Rise of the Modern Folk Song*. New York: Funk & Wagnall, 1962.

Brocken, Michael. *The British Folk Revival, 1944–2002*. Aldershot: Ashgate, 2003.

Brooks, Tim. *Lost Sounds: Blacks and the Birth of the Recording Industry, 1890–1919*. Urbana: University of Illinois Press, 2004.

Brower, Steve and Nora Guthrie. *Woody Guthrie: Art Works*. New York: Rizzoli, 2005.

Broyles, Michael. "Immigrant, Folk, and Regional Musics in the Nineteenth Century." In *The Cambridge History of American Music*, edited by David Nicholls, pp. 135–157. Cambridge: Cambridge University Press, 1998.

Brunning, Bob. *Blues: The British Connection*. London: Helter Skelter Publishing, 2002.

Brunvand, Jan Harold, ed. *American Folklore: An Encyclopedia*. New York: Garland Publishing, 1996.

Buchan, David. *The Ballad and the Folk*. London: Routledge & Kegan Paul, 1972.

Campbell, Gavin J. *Music & the Making of a New South*. Chapel Hill: University of North Carolina Press, 2004.

Cantwell, Robert. *Ethnomimesis: Folklife and the Representation of Culture*. Chapel Hill: University of North Carolina Press, 1993.

Cantwell, Robert. *When We Were Good: The Folk Revival*. Cambridge: Harvard University Press, 1996.

Carlin, Bob. *String Bands in the North Carolina Piedmont*. Jefferson, NC: McFarland & Company, 2004.

Carlin, Richard. *American Popular Music: Folk*. New York: Facts On File, 2005.

Cash, Johnny. *Cash: The Autobiography*. New York: HarperSan Francisco, 1997.

Cauthen, Joyce. *With Fiddle and Well Rosined Bow*. Tuscaloosa: University of Alabama Press, 1989.

Charters, Samuel B. *The Country Blues*. New York: Rinehart & Company, 1959.

Clancy, Liam. *The Mountain of the Women: Memoirs of an Irish Troubadour*. New York: Doubleday, 2002.

Clayton, Lawrence and Joe Specht, eds. *The Roots of Texas Music*. College Station: Texas A & M University Press, 2003.

Cohen, David. *Phil Ochs: A Bio-Bibliography*. Westport: Greenwood Press, 1999.

Cohen, Norm. *Folk Music: A Regional Exploration*. Westport: Greenwood Press, 2005.

Cohen, Ronald D., ed. *"Wasn't That A Time!": Firsthand Accounts of the Folk Music Revival*. Metuchen: Scarecrow Press, 1995.

Cohen, Ronald D. *Rainbow Quest: The Folk Music Revival and American Society, 1940–1970*. Amherst: University of Massachusetts Press, 2002.

Cohen, Ronald D., ed. *Alan Lomax: Selected Writings, 1934–1997*. New York: Routledge, 2003.

Cohn, Lawrence, ed. *Nothing But the Blues: The Music and the Musicians*. New York: Abbeville Press, 1993.

Collins, Shirley. *America Over the Water*. London: SAF Publishing, 2004.

Conway, Cecilia. *African Banjo Echoes in Appalachia: A Study of Folk Traditions*. Knoxville: University of Tennessee Press, 1995.

Cox, John H. *Folk-Songs of the South*. Cambridge: Harvard University Press, 1925.

Cray, Ed. *The Erotic Muse: American Bawdy Songs*. Urbana: University of Illinois Press, 1992.

Cray, Ed. *Ramblin' Man: The Life and Times of Woody Guthrie*. New York: W. W. Norton & Co., 2004.

Croft, Andy, ed. *A Weapon in the Struggle: The Cultural History of the Communist Party in Britain*. London: Pluto Press, 1998.

Crosby, David and Carl Gottlieb. *Long Time Gone: The Autobiography of David Crosby*. New York: Dell Publishing, 1998.

Crosby, David and David Bender. *Stand and Be Counted: Making Music, Making History*. New York: HarperSanFrancisco, 2000.

Cunningham, Agnes "Sis" and Gordon Friesen. *Red Dust and Broadsides: A Joint Autobiography*. Amherst: University of Massachusetts Press, 1999.

Darden, Robert. *People Get Ready! A New History of Black Gospel Music*. New York: Continuum, 2004.

Davis, Francis. *The History of the Blues*. New York: Hyperion, 1995.

Denisoff, R. Serge. *Great Day Coming: Folk Music and the American Left*. Urbana: University of Illinois Press, 1971.

Denning, Michael. *The Cultural Front: The Laboring of American Culture in the Twentieth Century*. New York: Verso, 1996.

Denver, John. *Take Me Home: An Autobiography*. New York: Harmony Books, 1994.

DeTurke, David, and A. Poulin, eds. *The American Folk Scene: Dimensions of the Folksong Revival*. New York: Dell Publishing, 1967.

Dewe, Michael. *The Skiffle Craze*. Aberystwyth: Planet, 1998.

Doerflinger, William. *Shantymen and Shantyboys: Songs of the Sailor and Lumberman*. New York: MacMillan, 1951.

Donleavy, Kevin. *Strings of Life: Conversations with Old-Time Musicians from Virginia and North Carolina*. Blacksburg: Pocahontas Press, 2004.

Dorson, Richard. *The British Folklorists: A History*. Chicago: University of Chicago Press, 1968.

Duberman, Martin. *Paul Robeson*. New York: Alfred A. Knopf, 1988.

Dunaway, David King. *How Can I Keep from Singing: Pete Seeger*. New York: McGraw-Hill, 1981.

Dunson, Josh. *Freedom in the Air: Song Movements of the Sixties*. New York: International Publishers, 1965.

Dylan, Bob. *Chronicles: Volume One*. New York: Simon & Schuster, 2004.

Edwards, David Honeyboy. *The World Don't Owe Me Nothing: The Life and Times of Delta Bluesman Honeyboy Edwards*. Chicago: Chicago Review Press, 1997.

Epstein, Dena J. *Sinful Tunes and Spirituals: Black Folk Music to the Civil War*. Urbana: University of Illinois Press, 1977.

Eyerman, Ron and Andrew Jamison. *Music and Social Movements: Mobilizing Traditions in the Twentieth Century*. New York: Cambridge University Press, 1998.

Filene, Benjamin. *Romancing the Folk: Public Memory & American Roots Music*. Chapel Hill: University of North Carolina Press, 2000.

Foner, Philip S. *American Labor Songs of the Nineteenth Century*. Urbana: University of Illinois Press, 1975.

Fuss, Charles J. *Joan Baez: A Bio-Bibliography*. Westport: Greenwood Press, 1996.

Gaar, Gillian. *She's a Rebel: The History of Women in Rock & Roll*. Seattle: Seal Press, 1992.

Gahr, David and Robert Shelton. *The Face of Folk Music*. New York: Citadel Press, 1968.

Gibson, Bob and Carole Bender. *I Come for to Sing: The Stops Along the Way of a Folk Music Legend*. Naperville, IL: Kingston Korner, 1999.

Glazer, Joe. *Labor's Troubadour*. Urbana: University of Illinois Press, 2001.

Glover, Tony, Scott Dirks, and Ward Gaines. *Blues with a Feeling: The Little Walter Story*. New York: Routledge, 2002.

Goldsmith, Peter D. *Making People's Music: Moe Asch and Folkways Records*. Washington: Smithsonian Institution Press, 1998.

Gordon, Robert. *Can't Be Satisfied: The Life and Times of Muddy Waters*. Boston: Little, Brown and Company, 2002.

Gordon, Robert and Bruce Nemerov, eds. *Lost Delta Found: Rediscovering the Fisk University–Library of Congress Coahoma County Study, 1941–1942*. Nashville: Vanderbilt University Press, 2005.

Green, Archie. *Torching the Fink Books and Other Essays on Vernacular Culture*. Chapel Hill: University of North Carolina Press, 2001.

Green, Douglas B. *Singing in the Saddle: The History of the Singing Cowboy*. Nashville: The Country Music Foundation Press and Vanderbilt University Press, 2002.

Greene, Victor. *A Passion for Polka: Old-Time Ethnic Music in America*. Berkeley: University of California Press, 1992.

Greene, Victor. *A Singing Ambivalence: American Immigrants Between Old World and New, 1830–1930*. Kent: Kent State University Press, 2004.

Greenway, John. *American Folk Songs of Protest*. Philadelphia: University of Pennsylvania Press, 1953.

Griffith, Nanci and Joe Jackson. *Nanci Griffith's Other Voices: A Personal History of Folk Music*. New York: Three Rivers Press, 1998.

Groom, Bob. *The Blues Revival*. London: Studio Vista, 1971.

Gura, Philip F. *C.F. Martin and His Guitars, 1796–1873*. Chapel Hill: University of North Carolina Press, 2003.

Gura, Philip F. and James F. Bollman. *America's Instrument: The Banjo in the Nineteenth Century*. Chapel Hill: University of North Carolina Press, 1991.

Guthrie, Woody. *Bound for Glory*. New York: E.P. Dutton, 1943.

Hajdu, David. *Positively 4th Street: The Lives and Times of Joan Baez, Bob Dylan, Mimi Baez Fariña and Richard Fariña*. New York: Farrar, Straus and Giroux, 2001.

Halker, Clark. *For Democracy, Workers, and God: Labor Song-Poems and Labor Protest, 1865–1895*. Urbana: University of Illinois Press, 1991.

Harkins, Anthony. *Hillbilly: A Cultural History of an American Icon*. New York: Oxford University Press, 2004.

Harris, Craig. *The New Folk Music*. Crown Point: White Cliffs Media Company, 1991.

Hart, Mickey. *Songcatchers: In Search of the World's Music*. Washington, D.C.: National Geographic, 2003.

Harvey, Todd. *The Formative Dylan: Transmission and Stylistic Influences, 1961–1963*. Lanham, MD: Scarecrow Press, 2001.

Haslam, Gerald W. *Workin' Man Blues: Country Music in California*. Berkeley: University of California Press, 1999.

Havens, Richie. *They Can't Hide Us Anymore*. New York: Avon Books, 1999.

Hirsch, Jerrold. *Portrait of America: A Cultural History of the Federal Writers' Project*. Chapel Hill: University of North Carolina Press, 2003.

Hoffmann, Frank, ed. *Encyclopedia of Recorded Sound*. 2 vols. New York: Routledge, 2005.

Holzman, Jac and Gavan Daws. *Follow the Music: The Life and High Times of Elektra Records in the Great Years of American Pop Culture*. Santa Monica: FirstMedia Books, 1998.

Jackson, Jerma A. *Singing in My Soul: Black Gospel Music in a Secular Age*. Chapel Hill: University of North Carolina Press, 2004.

Jaffe, Nina. *A Voice for the People: The Life and Work of Harold Courlander*. New York: Henry Holt and Company, 1997.

Jones, Loyal. *Minstrel of the Appalachians: The Story of Bascom Lamar Lunsford*. Boone, NC: Appalachian Consortium Press, 1984.

Kennedy, Rod. *Music from the Heart: The Fifty-Year Chronicle of His Life in Music*. Austin: Eakin Press, 1998.

Kingman, Daniel. *American Music: A Panorama*. New York: Schirmer Books, 1990.

Kingsbury, Paul, ed. *Country: The Music and the Musicians*. New York: Abbeville Press, 1994.

Kodish, Debora. *Good Friends and Bad Enemies: Robert Winslow Gordon and the Study of American Folksong*. Urbana: University of Illinois Press, 1986.

Koppelman, Robert S., ed. *Sing Out, Warning! Sing Out, Love!: The Writings of Lee Hays*. Amherst: University of Massachusetts Press, 2003.

Koskoff, Ellen, ed. *The Garland Encyclopedia of World Music, Vol. 3: The United States and Canada*. New York: Garland Publishing, 2001.

Krehbiel, Henry E. *Afro-American Folksongs: A Study in Racial and National Music*. New York: G. Schirmer, 1914.

Laing, Dave Karl Dallas, Robin Denslow, and Robert Shelton. *The Electric Muse: The Story of Folk into Rock*. London: Methuen, 1975.

Laing, Dave, and Richard Newman, eds. *Thirty Years of the Cambridge Folk Festval: The Definitive History of the World's Premier Acoustic Music Event*. Cambs: Music Maker Books, 1994.

Laird, Tracey W. *Louisiana Hayride: Radio and Roots Music Along the Red River*. New York: Oxford University Press, 2005.

Lange, Jeffrey J. *Smile When You Call Me a Hillbilly: Country Music's Struggle for Respectability, 1939–1954*. Athens: University of Georgia, 2004.

Lawless, Ray M. *Folksingers and Folksongs in America*. New York: Duell, Sloan and Pearce, 1965.

Laws, G. Malcolm. *American Balladry from British Broadsides*. Philadelphia: The American Folklore Society, 1957.

Laws, G. Malcolm. *Native American Balladry*. Philadelphia: The American Folklore Society, 1950.

Leach, MacEdward, ed. *The Ballad Book*. New York: A.S. Barnes & Company, 1955.

Leitch, Donovan. *The Autobiography of Donovan*. New York: St. Martin's Press, 2005.

Lieberman, Robbie. *"My Song Is My Weapon": People's Songs, American Communism, and the Politics of Culture, 1930–1950*. Urbana: University of Illinois Press, 1989.

Lifton, Sarah. *The Listener's Guide to Folk Music*. New York: Facts On File, 1983.

Linn, Karen. *That Half-Barbaric Twang: The Banjo in American Popular Culture*. Urbana: University of Illinois Press, 1991.

Lloyd, A. L. *Folk Song in England*. London: Lawrence & Wishart, 1967.

Logsdon, Guy. *"The Whorehouse Bells Were Ringing" and Other Songs Cowboys Sing*. Urbana: University of Illinois Press, 1989.

Lomax, Alan. *The Land Where the Blues Began*. New York: Pantheon Books, 1993.

Lomax, Alan. In *Selected Writings, 1934–1997*. Ronald D. Cohen, ed., New York: Routledge, 2003.

Lomax, John A. *Cowboy Songs and Other Frontier Ballads*. New York: Sturgis & Walton, 1917.

Lomax, John A. *Adventures of a Ballad Hunter*. New York: MacMillan, 1947.

Lomax, John A. and Alan Lomax. *American Ballads and Folk Songs*. New York: MacMillan, 1934.

Lomax, John A. and Alan Lomax. *Negro Folk Songs as Sung by Lead Belly*. New York: MacMillan, 1936.

Lomax, John A. and Alan Lomax. *Cowboy Songs and Other Frontier Ballads*. Revised and enlarged. New York: MacMillan Company, 1938.

Lomax, John A., and Alan Lomax. *Our Singing Country: A Second Volume of American Ballads and Folk Songs*. New York: MacMillan, 1941.

Lomax, John A., and Alan Lomax. *Best Loved American Folk Songs*. New York: Grosset & Dunlap, 1947.

Longhi, Jim. *Woody, Cisco, & Me: Seamen Three in the Merchant Marine*. Urbana: University of Illinois Press, 1997.

Lornell, Kip. *Introducing American Folk Music.* Madison: Brown & Benchmark, 1993.

Lornell, Kip. *The NPR Curious Listener's Guide to American Folk Music.* New York: Perigee Books, 2004.

Lynch, Timothy P. *Strike Songs of the Depression.* Jackson: University Press of Mississippi, 2001.

MacColl, Ewan. *Journeyman: An Autobiography.* London: Sidgwick & Jackson, 1990.

MacKinnon, Niall. *The British Folk Scene: Musical Performance and Social Identity.* Buckingham: Open University Press, 1994.

Malone, Bill C. *Country Music U.S.A.* Rev. ed. Austin: University of Texas Press, 1985.

Malone, Bill C. *Singing Cowboys and Musical Mountaineers.* Athens: University of Georgia Press, 1993.

.Malone, Bill C. *Don't Get Above Your Raisin': Country Music and the Southern Working Class.* Urbana: University of Illinois Press, 2002.

Malone, Bill C. and David Stricklin. *Southern Music/American Music.* Rev. ed. Lexington: University Press of Kentucky, 2003.

Malone, Bill C. and Judith McCulloh, eds. *Stars of Country Music: Uncle Dave Macon to Johnny Rodriguez.* Urbana: University of Illinois Press, 1975.

McCusker, Kristine M. and Diane Pecknold, eds. *A Boy Named Sue: Gender and Country Music.* Jackson: University Press of Mississippi, 2004.

McDevitt, Chas. *Skiffle: The Definitive Inside Story.* London: Robson Books, 1997.

McGee, Marty. *Traditional Musicians of the Central Blue Ridge.* Jefferson, NC: McFarland & Company, 2000.

Metting, Fred. *The Unbroken Circle: Tradition and Innovation in the Music of Ry Cooder and Taj Mahal.* Lanham, MD: Scarecrow Press, 2001.

Miller, Terry E. *Folk Music in America: A Reference Guide.* New York: Garland Publishing, 1986.

Milnes, Gerald. *Play of a Fiddle: Traditional Music, Dance, and Folklore in West Virginia*. Lexington: University Press of Kentucky, 1999.

Munro, Ailie. *The Democratic Muse: Folk Music Revival in Scotland*. Aberdeen: Scottish Cultural Press, 1996.

Murray, Charles Shaar. *Boogie Man: The Adventures of John Lee Hooker in the American Twentieth Century*. New York: St. Martin's Press, 2000.

Near, Holly. *Fire in the Rain, Singer in the Storm: An Autobiography*. New York: William Morrow, 1990.

Odum, Howard W. and Guy B. Johnson, eds. *The Negro and His Songs: A Study of Typical Negro Songs in the South*. Chapel Hill: University of North Carolina Press, 1925.

Oermann, Robert K. *A Century of Country Music: An Illustrated History of Country Music*. New York: TV Books, 1999.

Oliver, Paul. *The Story of the Blues*. Philadelphia: Chilton Book Company, 1969.

Oliver, Paul, Max Harrison, and William Bolcom. *The New Grove Gospel, Blues and Jazz*. New York: W.W. Norton, 1986.

Oster, Harry. *Living Country Blues*. Detroit: Folklore Associates, 1969.

Perone, James. *Songs of the Vietnam Conflict*. Westport: Greenwood Press, 2001.

Perone, James. *Music of the Counterculture Era*. Westport: Greenwood Press, 2004.

Pescatello, Ann M. *Charles Seeger: A Life in American Music*. Pittsburgh: University of Pittsburgh Press, 1992.

Phillips, John. *Papa John: An Autobiography*. New York: Dell, 1986.

Pickering, Michael. *Village Song & Culture: A Study Based on the Blunt Collection of Song from Adderbury North Oxfordshire*. London: Croom Helm, 1982.

Pickering, Michael and Tony Green, eds. *Everyday Culture: Popular Song and the Vernacular Milieu*. Milton Keynes: Open University Press, 1987.

Plantenga, Bart. *Yodel-Ay-Eo-Oooo: The Secret History of Yodeling around the World*. New York: Routledge, 2004.

Porterfield, Nolan. *Jimmie Rodgers: The Life and Times of America's Blue Yodeler*. Urbana: University of Illinois Press, 1979.

Porterfield, Nolan. *Last Cavalier: The Life and Times of John A. Lomax, 1867–1948*. Urbana: University of Illinois Press, 1996.

Porterfield, Nolan, ed. *Exploring Roots Music: Twenty Years of the JEMF Quarterly*. Lanham: Scarecrow Press, 2004.

Post, Jennifer C. *Music in Rural New England Family and Community Life, 1870–1940*. Hanover: University Press of New England, 2004.

Ramsey, Frederic. *Been Here and Gone*. New Brunswick: Rutgers University Press, 1960.

Randolph, Vance. *Ozark Folksongs*. Columbia: Historical Society of Missouri, 4 vols., 1980.

Randolph, Vance. *Roll Me in Your Arms: "Unprintable" Ozark Folksongs and Folklore* (vol. 1: Folksongs and Music) and *Blow the Candle Out* (vol. 2: Folk Rhymes and Other Lore). Fayetteville: University of Arkansas Press, 1992.

Reuss, Richard A. and JoAnne C. Reuss. *American Folk Music and Left-Wing Politics, 1927–1957*. Lanham: The Scarecrow Press, 2000.

Romalis, Shelly. *Pistol Packin' Mama: Aunt Molly Jackson and the Politics of Folksong*. Urbana: University of Illinois Press, 1999.

Roscigno, Vincent J. and William F. Danaher. *The Voice of Southern Labor: Radio, Music, and Textile Strikes, 1929–1934*. Minneapolis: University of Minnesota Press, 2004.

Rosenberg, Neil V., ed. *Transforming Tradition: Folk Music Revivals Examined*. Urbana: University of Illinois Press, 1993.

Rouse, Andrew C. *The Remunerated Vernacular Singer: From Medieval England to the Post-War Revival*. New York: Peter Lang, 2005.

Russell, Ian, ed. *Singer, Song and Scholar*. Sheffield: Sheffield Academic Press, 1986.

Russell, Ian and David Atkinson, eds. *Folk Song: Tradition, Revival, and Re-Creation*. Aberdeen: The Elphinstone Institute, University of Aberdeen, 2004.

San Miguel, Guadalupe. *Tejano Proud: Tex-Mex Music in the Twentieth Century*. College Station: Texas A & M University Press, 2002.

Sandberg, Larry and Dick Weissman. *The Folk Music Sourcebook*. New York: Da Capo, 1989.

Sandburg, Carl. *The American Songbag*. New York: Harcourt Brace, 1927.

Sanders, Lynn Moss. *And Howard W. Odum's Folklore Odyssey: Transformation to Tolerance Through African American Folk Studies*. Athens: University of Georgia Press, 2003.

Santelli, Robert, Holly George-Warren, and Jim Brown, eds. *American Roots Music*. New York: Harry N. Abrams, 2001.

Santelli, Robert, and Emily Davidson, eds. *Hard Travelin': The Life and Legacy of Woody Guthrie*. Hanover: University Press of New England, 1999.

Santoro, Gene. *Highway 61 Revisited: The Tangled Roots of American Jazz, Blues, Rock and Country Music*. New York: Oxford University Press, 2004.

Scarborough, Dorothy. *On the Trail of Negro Folk-Songs*. Cambridge: Harvard University Press, 1925.

Schumacher, Michael. *There But for Fortune: The Life of Phil Ochs*. New York: Hyperion, 1996.

Seeger, Peggy. *The Peggy Seeger Songbook: Warts and All: Forty Years of Songmaking*. New York: Oak Publications, 1998.

Seeger, Peggy, comp. *The Essential Ewan MacColl Songbook: Sixty Years of Songmaking*. New York: Oak Publications, 2001.

Segrest, James and Mark Hoffman. *Moanin' at Midnight: The Life and Times of Howlin' Wolf*. New York: Pantheon Books, 2004.

Seward, Theodore F., ed. *Jubilee Songs as Sung by the Fisk Jubilee Singers*. New York: Bigelow and Main, 1872.

Sharp, Cecil J., ed. *One Hundred English Folksongs*. Philadelphia: Oliver Ditson, 1916.

Shelton, Robert. *No Direction Home: The Life and Music of Bob Dylan*. New York: Beech Tree Books, 1986.

Slobin, Mark. *Tenement Songs: The Popular Music of the Jewish Immigrants*. Urbana: University of Illinois Press, 1982.

Smith, Ralph Lee and Madeline MacNeil. *Folk Songs of Old Kentucky*. Pacific, MO: Mel Bay Publications, 2003.

Smith, Richard. *Can't You Hear Me Callin': The Life of Bill Monroe, Father of Bluegrass*. Boston: Little, Brown and Company, 2000.

Sounes, Howard. *Down the Highway: The Life of Bob Dylan*. New York: Grove Press, 2001.

Southern, Eileen. *The Music of Black Americans: A History*. New York: W.W. Norton, 1971.

Spitz, Bob. *Dylan: A Biography*. New York: McGraw-Hill, 1989.

Stambler, Irwin and Grelun Landon. *The Encyclopedia of Folk, Country & Western Music*. New York: St. Martin's Press, 1984.

Stambler, Irwin and Lyndon Stambler. *Folk and Blues: The Encyclopedia*. New York: St. Martin's Press, 2001.

Star, Larry and Christopher Waterman. *American Popular Music: From Minstrelsy to MTV*. New York: Oxford University Press, 2003.

Sweers, Britta. *Electric Folk: The Changing Face of English Traditional Music*. New York: Oxford University Press, 2005.

Thorp, Jack. *Songs of the Cowboy*. Estancia, NM: Jack Thorp, 1908.

Tick, Judith. *Ruth Crawford Seeger: A Composer's Search for American Music*. New York: Oxford University Press, 1997.

Titon, Jeff Todd and Bob Carlin, eds. *American Musical Traditions*. 5 vols. New York: Schirmer Reference, 2002.

Tribe, Ivan M. *The Stonemans: An Appalachian Family and the Music That Shaped Their Lives*. Urbana: University of Illinois Press, 1993.

Unterberger, Richie. *Turn! Turn! Turn!: The '60s Folk-Rock Revolution*. San Francisco: Backbeat Books, 2002.

Unterberger, Richie. *Eight Miles High: Folk-Rock's Flight from Haight-Ashbury to Woodstock*. San Francisco: Backbeat Books, 2003.

Van Der Horst, Brian. *Folk Music in America*. New York: Franklin Watts, 1972.

Van der Tuuk, Alex. *Paramount's Rise and Fall: A History of the Wisconsin Chair Company and Its Recording Activities*. Denver: Mainspring Press, 2003.

Van Rijn, Guido. *Roosevelt's Blues: African American Blues and Gospel Songs on FDR*. Jackson: University Press of Mississippi, 1997.

Van Rijn, Guido. *The Truman and Eisenhower Blues: African American Blues and Gospel Songs, 1945–1960*. London: Continuum, 2004.

Van Ronk, Dave and Elijah Wald. *The Mayor of MacDougal Street: A Memoir*. Cambridge: Da Capo, 2005.

Von Schmidt, Eric and Jim Rooney. *Baby, Let Me Follow You Down: The Illustrated Story of the Cambridge Folk Years*. New York: Anchor Books, 1979.

Wald, Elijah. *Josh White: Society Blues*. Amherst: University of Massachusetts Press, 2000.

Wald, Elijah. *Narcocorrido: A Journey into the Music of Drugs, Guns, and Guerrillas*. New York: HarperCollins Publishers, 2001.

Wald, Elijah. *Escaping the Delta: Robert Johnson and the Invention of the Blues*. New York: Amistad, 2004.

Walters, Neal and Brian Mansfield, eds. *Music Hound Folk: The Essential Album Guide*. Detroit: Visible Ink, 1998.

Ward, Brian. *Just My Soul Responding: Rhythm and Blues, Black Consciousness, and Race Relations*. Berkeley: University of California Press, 1998.

Wardlow, Gayle Dean. *Chasin' That Devil Music: Searching for the Blues*. San Francisco: Backbeat Books, 1998.

Wein, George and Nate Chinen. *Myself Among Others: A Life in Music*. New York: Da Capo, 2003.

Weissman, Dick. *Blues: The Basics*. New York: Routledge, 2005(a).

Weissman, Dick. *Which Side Are You On? An Inside History of the Folk Music Revival in America*. New York: Continuum, 2005(b).

Whisnant, David E. *All That Is Native & Fine: The Politics of Culture in an American Region*. Chapel Hill: University of North Carolina Press, 1983.

White, Newman I. *American Negro Folk-Songs*. Cambridge: Harvard University Press, 1928.

Wiggins, Gene. *Fiddlin' Georgia Crazy: Fiddlin' John Carson, His Real World, and the World of His Songs*. Urbana: University of Illinois Press, 1987.

Wilentz, Sean, and Greil Marcus, eds. *The Rose and the Briar*. New York: W.W. Norton, 2004.

Wilgus, D.K. *Anglo-American Folksong Scholarship Since 1898*. New Brunswick: Rutgers University Press, 1959.

Willens, Doris. *Lonesome Traveler: The Life of Lee Hays*. New York: W.W. Norton, 1988.

Williams, William H. A. *'Twas Only an Irishman's Dream: The Image of Ireland and the Irish in American Popular Song Lyrics, 1800–1920*. Urbana: University of Illinois Press, 1996.

Wolfe, Charles K. *A Good-Natured Riot: The Birth of the Grand Ole Opry*. Nashville: The Country Music Foundation Press/Vanderbilt University Press, 1999.

Wolfe, Charles K. *Classic Country: Legends of Country Music*. New York: Routledge, 2001.

Wolfe, Charles K. and James E. Akenson, eds. *Country Music Goes to War*. Lexington: University Press of Kentucky, 2005.

Wolfe, Charles and Kip Lornell. *The Life and Legend of Leadbelly*. New York: HarperCollins, 1992.

Wolfe, Charles and Ted Olson, eds. *The Bristol Sessions: Writings about the Big Bang of Country Music*. Jefferson, NC: McFarland & Company, 2005.

Woliver, Robbie. *Bringing It All Back Home: Twenty-Five Years of American Music at Folk City*. New York: Pantheon Books, 1986.

Wolkin, Jan Mark, and Bill Keenom. *Michael Bloomfield: If You Love These Blues, An Oral History*. San Francisco: Miller Freeman Books, 2000.

Woods, Fred. *Folk Revival: The Rediscovery of a National Music*. Poole: Blandford Press, 1979.

Work, John W. and Frederick J. Work. *Folk Songs of the American Negro*. Nashville: The Authors, 1907.

Yates, Mike, Elaine Bradtke, and Malcolm Taylor, eds. *Dear Companion: Appalachian Traditional Songs and Singers from the Cecil Sharp Collection*. London: English Folk Dance & Song Society, 2004.

Zwonitzer, Mark and Charles Hirshberg. *Will You Miss Me When I'm Gone?: The Carter Family and Their Legacy in American Music*. New York: Simon & Schuster, 2002.

INDEX